English Questions:

Practice Drills in All

Active Tenses

....

JJ Polk

GLOBAL TOUCHSTONES

English Questions:
Practice Drills in All Active Tenses

Copyright © 2014 JJ Polk

All Rights Reserved. No part of this book may be reproduced in any form or by any means, electronic or mechanical, including photocopying, recording, or by any information storage and retrieval system, without permission in writing from the author and publisher.

ISBN: 978-0-9912014-0-2

Published by

Los Angeles, CA

Cover and interior design by Stacey Aaronson

Printed in the USA

CONTENTS

Preface 1

UNIT 1: QUESTIONS IN THE PRESENT SIMPLE 3

UNIT 2: QUESTIONS IN THE PRESENT PROGRESSIVE 15

UNIT 3: QUESTIONS IN THE PRESENT PERFECT 27

UNIT 4: QUESTIONS IN THE PRESENT PERFECT PROGRESSIVE 39

UNIT 5: QUESTIONS IN THE PAST SIMPLE 51

UNIT 6: QUESTIONS IN THE PAST PROGRESSIVE 62

UNIT 7: QUESTIONS IN THE PAST PERFECT 73

UNIT 8: QUESTIONS IN THE PAST PERFECT PROGRESSIVE 84

UNIT 9: QUESTIONS IN THE FUTURE SIMPLE 95

UNIT 10: QUESTIONS IN THE FUTURE PROGRESSIVE 106

UNIT 11: QUESTIONS IN THE FUTURE PERFECT 117

UNIT 12: QUESTIONS IN THE FUTURE PERFECT PROGRESSIVE 123

SKELETAL FORMS OF QUESTIONS IN ALL ACTIVE TENSES 129

About the Author 147

PREFACE

The variety of forms and usage patterns typically found in English questions pose particular challenges for non-native speakers, even for those at otherwise fairly advanced proficiency levels. *English Questions: Practice Drills in All Active Tenses* is conceived as a supplemental set of exercises to help intermediate and pre-advanced level students achieve greater mastery of the four major types of questions commonly used in everyday communication.

Emphasis has been given throughout the text solely to the grammar and syntax of questions in all active tenses, consciously at the expense of contextualized usage. Where possible, priority has also been given to spoken / colloquial forms as opposed to more stylized written patterns.

Instructors who might wish to use these practice activities in the classroom setting would naturally wish to pre-teach vocabulary elements that might be unfamiliar to the target students. It should also be noted, as is evident in the accompanying *Answer Key*, that questions of greater complexity involving both dependent and independent clauses often permit variations in word order that are fully acceptable.

UNIT 1

QUESTIONS IN THE PRESENT SIMPLE

DIRECTIONS: Transform each of the following sentences into the type of question required in each of the given blanks. The underlined phrases in each sentence indicate which question phrase should be used.

Example: I usually get up <u>at 7:30</u>.
Wh-question: What time do you usually get up?
Question tag type 1: You usually get up at 7:30, don't you? [expected positive response]
Question tag type 2: You don't usually get up at 7:30, do you? [expected negative response]
Yes / No question: Do you usually get up at 7:30?

1. Flight 405 to Chicago departs <u>at 4:45</u>.

Wh-question: _____

Question tag type 1: _____

Question tag type 2: _____

Yes / No question: _____

2. Phillip works <u>in Sydney, Australia</u>.

Wh-question: _____

Question tag type 1: _____

Question tag type 2: _____

Yes / No question: _____

3. Our company employs more than 30,000 people worldwide.

Wh-question: _____

Question tag type 1: _____

Question tag type 2: _____

Yes / No question: _____

4. Susan drives a blue car.

Wh-question: _____

Question tag type 1: _____

Question tag type 2: _____

Yes / No question: _____

5. The British prime minister lives at No. 10 Downing Street.

Wh-question: _____

Question tag type 1: _____

Question tag type 2: _____

Yes / No question: _____

6. We run training sessions every quarter.

Wh-question: _____

Question tag type 1: _____

Question tag type 2: _____

Yes / No question: _____

7. The Great Wall of China is more than 21,000 km long.

Wh-question: _____

Question tag type 1: _____

Question tag type 2: _____

Yes / No question: _____

UNIT 1 | QUESTIONS IN THE PRESENT SIMPLE

8. Beijing is the capital of China.

Wh-question: _____

Question tag type 1: _____

Question tag type 2: _____

Yes / No question: _____

9. The president of the United States lives in the White House.

Wh-question: _____

Question tag type 1: _____

Question tag type 2: _____

Yes / No question: _____

10. The White House is in Washington, D. C.

Wh-question: _____

Question tag type 1: _____

Question tag type 2: _____

Yes / No question: _____

11. Russia is the largest country in area.

Wh-question: _____

Question tag type 1: _____

Question tag type 2: _____

Yes / No question: _____

12. China has the largest population of any country.

Wh-question: _____

Question tag type 1: _____

Question tag type 2: _____

Yes / No question: _____

13. <u>English</u> is the most widely spoken language.

Wh-question: _____
Question tag type 1: _____
Question tag type 2: _____
Yes / No question: _____

14. The headquarters of the company is <u>in Munich, Germany</u>.

Wh-question: _____
Question tag type 1: _____
Question tag type 2: _____
Yes / No question: _____

15. Water freezes <u>at 0 ºC</u>.

Wh-question: _____
Question tag type 1: _____
Question tag type 2: _____
Yes / No question: _____

16. We usually stay <u>at the Burj Khalifa</u> when we're in Dubai.

Wh-question: _____
Question tag type 1: _____
Question tag type 2: _____
Yes / No question: _____

17. The bus runs <u>every 20 minutes</u>.

Wh-question: _____
Question tag type 1: _____
Question tag type 2: _____
Yes / No question: _____

UNIT 1 | QUESTIONS IN THE PRESENT SIMPLE

18. "GPS" stands for "global positioning system."

Wh-question: _____

Question tag type 1: _____

Question tag type 2: _____

Yes / No question: _____

19. We normally play tennis twice a week.

Wh-question: _____

Question tag type 1: _____

Question tag type 2: _____

Yes / No question: _____

20. The president of the United States earns more than $400,000 per year.

Wh-question: _____

Question tag type 1: _____

Question tag type 2: _____

Yes / No question: _____

21. This cell phone uses the Gamoid operating system.

Wh-question: _____

Question tag type 1: _____

Question tag type 2: _____

Yes / No question: _____

22. The cheapest rooms at this hotel are $150.00 per night.

Wh-question: _____

Question tag type 1: _____

Question tag type 2: _____

Yes / No question: _____

23. We charge $55.00 per kilo for excess baggage.

Wh-question: _____
Question tag type 1: _____
Question tag type 2: _____
Yes / No question: _____

24. This computer runs at a clock speed of 3.8 GHz.

Wh-question: _____
Question tag type 1: _____
Question tag type 2: _____
Yes / No question: _____

25. Our offices open at 8:30.

Wh-question: _____
Question tag type 1: _____
Question tag type 2: _____
Yes / No question: _____

26. Our hedge fund currently manages more than five billion in assets.

Wh-question: _____
Question tag type 1: _____
Question tag type 2: _____
Yes / No question: _____

27. The minimum English requirements for this position are a Cambridge "Advanced" level.

Wh-question: _____
Question tag type 1: _____
Question tag type 2: _____
Yes / No question: _____

UNIT 1 | QUESTIONS IN THE PRESENT SIMPLE

28. The corporation has <u>390</u> branch offices.

Wh-question: _____
Question tag type 1: _____
Question tag type 2: _____
Yes / No question: _____

29. Most of the company's manufacturing takes place <u>in the People's Republic of China</u>.

Wh-question: _____
Question tag type 1: _____
Question tag type 2: _____
Yes / No question: _____

30. This new model of hybrid car gets <u>52 miles per gallon</u>.

Wh-question: _____
Question tag type 1: _____
Question tag type 2: _____
Yes / No question: _____

31. The past tense of "smell" in American English is "<u>smelled</u>."

Wh-question: _____
Question tag type 1: _____
Question tag type 2: _____
Yes / No question: _____

32. I spell my last name "<u>H-i-g-g-e-n-b-o-t-h-a-m</u>."

Wh-question: _____
Question tag type 1: _____
Question tag type 2: _____
Yes / No question: _____

33. It normally takes <u>around five hours</u> to fly from New York to Los Angeles.

Wh-question: _____

Question tag type 1: _____

Question tag type 2: _____

Yes / No question: _____

34. <u>More than 36 million people</u> live in the greater Tokyo-Yokohama metropolitan area.

Wh-question: _____

Question tag type 1: _____

Question tag type 2: _____

Yes / No question: _____

35. <u>Airbus</u> makes the giant superjumbo A380.

Wh-question: _____

Question tag type 1: _____

Question tag type 2: _____

Yes / No question: _____

36. One liter of water weighs <u>one kilogram</u>.

Wh-question: _____

Question tag type 1: _____

Question tag type 2: _____

Yes / No question: _____

37. The Burj Khalifa is <u>828 meters tall</u>.

Wh-question: _____

Question tag type 1: _____

Question tag type 2: _____

Yes / No question: _____

38. Cave diving is the most dangerous sport.

Wh-question: _____

Question tag type 1: _____

Question tag type 2: _____

Yes / No question: _____

39. The word for this fruit in English is "watermelon."

Wh-question: _____

Question tag type 1: _____

Question tag type 2: _____

Yes / No question: _____

40. I generally like my coffee black with no sugar.

Wh-question: _____

Question tag type 1: _____

Question tag type 2: _____

Yes / No question: _____

41. We usually eat dinner at around 6:30.

Wh-question: _____

Question tag type 1: _____

Question tag type 2: _____

Yes / No question: _____

42. I get up so early because there's much less noise in the early morning hours.

Wh-question: _____

Question tag type 1: _____

Question tag type 2: _____

Yes / No question: _____

43. My sister lives in Cape Town, South Africa.

Wh-question: _____

Question tag type 1: _____

Question tag type 2: _____

Yes / No question: _____

44. It normally takes around six hours to drive from Los Angeles to San Francisco.

Wh-question: _____

Question tag type 1: _____

Question tag type 2: _____

Yes / No question: _____

45. My family normally goes on summer vacation in June.

Wh-question: _____

Question tag type 1: _____

Question tag type 2: _____

Yes / No question: _____

46. I have three brothers and two sisters.

Wh-question: _____

Question tag type 1: _____

Question tag type 2: _____

Yes / No question: _____

47. We travel to Europe twice a year.

Wh-question: _____

Question tag type 1: _____

Question tag type 2: _____

Yes / No question: _____

UNIT 1 | QUESTIONS IN THE PRESENT SIMPLE

48. <u>My mother</u> usually cooks at our house.

Wh-question: _____

Question tag type 1: _____

Question tag type 2: _____

Yes / No question: _____

49. I go swimming <u>once a week</u>.

Wh-question: _____

Question tag type 1: _____

Question tag type 2: _____

Yes / No question: _____

50. I live <u>in the eastern-most</u> part of the state.

Wh-question: _____

Question tag type 1: _____

Question tag type 2: _____

Yes / No question: _____

QUESTIONS WITH MODAL VERBS:

[Note on the use of modals in American English: Of the recognized modal verbs in English, only *can*, *could*, *should*, *will*, and *would* are commonly used in spoken American English in all the question forms practiced in this book. Other modals not listed here often experience shifts in meaning, or represent forms that are now widely regarded as archaic (e.g., "shall" and "shan't"). *Must* is rarely used in positive declarative statements to express emphatic obligation and has largely been replaced by an appropriate form of "have to," or alternatively, is rephrased with *subject + is / are + required to*. Note also that the negative form (*mustn't*) becomes prohibitive; its use in tag questions is thus limited.]

51. We can go <u>to Yellowstone</u> during summer vacation.

Wh-question: _____

Question tag type 1: _____

Question tag type 2: _____

Yes / No question: _____

52. Weijie should speak English in class.

Wh-question: _____
Question tag type 1: _____
Question tag type 2: _____
Yes / No question: _____

53. I would buy the tickets now.

Wh-question: _____
Question tag type 1: _____
Question tag type 2: _____
Yes / No question: _____

54. Tim could help with the cooking.

Wh-question: _____
Question tag type 1: _____
Question tag type 2: _____
Yes / No question: _____

55. You may use room 910 for your debate.

Wh-question: _____
Question tag type 1: _____
Question tag type 2: _____
Yes / No question: _____

56. Stephanie could be at her cousin's house.

Wh-question: _____
Question tag type 1: _____
Question tag type 2: _____
Yes / No question: _____

UNIT 2

QUESTIONS IN THE PRESENT PROGRESSIVE

DIRECTIONS: Transform each of the following sentences into the type of question required in each of the given blanks. The underlined phrases in each sentence indicate which question phrase should be used.

Example: *I am swimming.*
Wh-question: *What are you doing?*
Question tag type 1:   *You're swimming, aren't you?* [expected positive response]
Question tag type 2:   *You aren't swimming, are you?* [expected negative response]
Yes / No question: *Are you swimming?*

1. Tom and Jamilla are playing tennis.

Wh-question: _____

Question tag type 1: _____

Question tag type 2: _____

Yes / No question: _____

2. Flight 633 to Hong Kong is boarding at Gate 5.

Wh-question: _____

Question tag type 1: _____

Question tag type 2: _____

Yes / No question: _____

3. I'm having dinner near the Arc de Triomphe.

Wh-question: _____

Question tag type 1: _____

Question tag type 2: _____

Yes / No question: _____

4. We're sending out 200 invitations to the wedding ceremony.

Wh-question: _____

Question tag type 1: _____

Question tag type 2: _____

Yes / No question: _____

5. We're writing a protest letter to the ambassador.

Wh-question: _____

Question tag type 1: _____

Question tag type 2: _____

Yes / No question: _____

6. My aunt is taking aspirin.

Wh-question: _____

Question tag type 1: _____

Question tag type 2: _____

Yes / No question: _____

7. Suzanne and Kathy are playing volleyball at the beach.

Wh-question: _____

Question tag type 1: _____

Question tag type 2: _____

Yes / No question: _____

UNIT 2 | QUESTIONS IN THE PRESENT PROGRESSIVE

8. Jack is trying to <u>complete the crossword puzzle</u> in the newspaper.

Wh-question: _____

Question tag type 1: _____

Question tag type 2: _____

Yes / No question: _____

9. Carla is studying <u>French literature</u> at the university.

Wh-question: _____

Question tag type 1: _____

Question tag type 2: _____

Yes / No question: _____

10. I'm having dinner <u>with friends</u>.

Wh-question: _____

Question tag type 1: _____

Question tag type 2: _____

Yes / No question: _____

11. We're sending these letters <u>to England</u>.

Wh-question: _____

Question tag type 1: _____

Question tag type 2: _____

Yes / No question: _____

12. Rachel and her husband are building a new house <u>on the south side of Lake Tahoe</u>.

Wh-question: _____

Question tag type 1: _____

Question tag type 2: _____

Yes / No question: _____

13. Janet is <u>practicing the flute</u>.

Wh-question: _____

Question tag type 1: _____

Question tag type 2: _____

Yes / No question: _____

14. <u>A snake</u> is crawling out of the pile of brush.

Wh-question: _____

Question tag type 1: _____

Question tag type 2: _____

Yes / No question: _____

15. The two men are trying <u>to break into the car</u>.

Wh-question: _____

Question tag type 1: _____

Question tag type 2: _____

Yes / No question: _____

16. <u>The country's most famous lawyer</u> is defending the alleged kidnapper.

Wh-question: _____

Question tag type 1: _____

Question tag type 2: _____

Yes / No question: _____

17. Ms. Myers is performing <u>the Barber violin concerto</u>.

Wh-question: _____

Question tag type 1: _____

Question tag type 2: _____

Yes / No question: _____

18. Ms. Myers is performing the Barber violin concerto.

Wh-question: _____

Question tag type 1: _____

Question tag type 2: _____

Yes / No question: _____

19. Cynthia is taking golf lessons twice a week.

Wh-question: _____

Question tag type 1: _____

Question tag type 2: _____

Yes / No question: _____

20. Charlotte is downloading five more textbooks to prepare for her medical exams.

Wh-question: _____

Question tag type 1: _____

Question tag type 2: _____

Yes / No question: _____

21. James is studying Hebrew because he wants to become a theologian.

Wh-question: _____

Question tag type 1: _____

Question tag type 2: _____

Yes / No question: _____

22. They're trying to stop the leak with a thick wad of chewing gum.

Wh-question: _____

Question tag type 1: _____

Question tag type 2: _____

Yes / No question: _____

23. Jessie is analyzing the data <u>using a common statistics program</u>.

Wh-question: _____
Question tag type 1: _____
Question tag type 2: _____
Yes / No question: _____

24. Benjamin is <u>taking a helicopter</u> into Manhattan from the airport.

Wh-question: _____
Question tag type 1: _____
Question tag type 2: _____
Yes / No question: _____

25. The dealer is asking <u>$55,000</u> for the collectors' edition of the camera.

Wh-question: _____
Question tag type 1: _____
Question tag type 2: _____
Yes / No question: _____

26. <u>Four thousand</u> guests are attending the outdoor concert.

Wh-question: _____
Question tag type 1: _____
Question tag type 2: _____
Yes / No question: _____

27. <u>Khalid</u> is leading the discussion.

Wh-question: _____
Question tag type 1: _____
Question tag type 2: _____
Yes / No question: _____

UNIT 2 | QUESTIONS IN THE PRESENT PROGRESSIVE

28. <u>Samantha</u> is running for city council.

Wh-question: _____

Question tag type 1: _____

Question tag type 2: _____

Yes / No question: _____

29. <u>An incoming train</u> is making that loud noise.

Wh-question: _____

Question tag type 1: _____

Question tag type 2: _____

Yes / No question: _____

30. <u>A blast of Arctic air</u> is causing this freeze.

Wh-question: _____

Question tag type 1: _____

Question tag type 2: _____

Yes / No question: _____

31. The state is holding special elections <u>today</u>.

Wh-question: _____

Question tag type 1: _____

Question tag type 2: _____

Yes / No question: _____

32. The professor is answering questions from the audience <u>after the break</u>.

Wh-question: _____

Question tag type 1: _____

Question tag type 2: _____

Yes / No question: _____

33. Sam and his wife are vacationing in the Caribbean.

Wh-question: _____
Question tag type 1: _____
Question tag type 2: _____
Yes / No question: _____

34. The lead investigator is answering questions from the public.

Wh-question: _____
Question tag type 1: _____
Question tag type 2: _____
Yes / No question: _____

35. The astrophysicists are calculating the asteroid's path with a supercomputer.

Wh-question: _____
Question tag type 1: _____
Question tag type 2: _____
Yes / No question: _____

36. That woman is betting $2,000 on her favorite horse.

Wh-question: _____
Question tag type 1: _____
Question tag type 2: _____
Yes / No question: _____

37. My sister is playing football every weekend.

Wh-question: _____
Question tag type 1: _____
Question tag type 2: _____
Yes / No question: _____

UNIT 2 | QUESTIONS IN THE PRESENT PROGRESSIVE

38. My girlfriend is reading *Anna Karenina* to prepare for her literature exam.

Wh-question: _____
Question tag type 1: _____
Question tag type 2: _____
Yes / No question: _____

39. They're building their house on stilts to prevent possible flood damage.

Wh-question: _____
Question tag type 1: _____
Question tag type 2: _____
Yes / No question: _____

40. Hiroaki is dating someone from Nagoya.

Wh-question: _____
Question tag type 1: _____
Question tag type 2: _____
Yes / No question: _____

41. Mary is unfriending her roommate because of a bad argument.

Wh-question: _____
Question tag type 1: _____
Question tag type 2: _____
Yes / No question: _____

42. My boss is texting me about the company trip next week.

Wh-question: _____
Question tag type 1: _____
Question tag type 2: _____
Yes / No question: _____

43. The two students in the hall are speaking <u>Romansch</u>.

Wh-question: _____

Question tag type 1: _____

Question tag type 2: _____

Yes / No question: _____

44. My nephew is teaching <u>Korean</u> at the local community college.

Wh-question: _____

Question tag type 1: _____

Question tag type 2: _____

Yes / No question: _____

45. My parents are staying <u>at the Peninsula Hotel</u> while they're in Hong Kong.

Wh-question: _____

Question tag type 1: _____

Question tag type 2: _____

Yes / No question: _____

46. The Chens are celebrating their wedding anniversary <u>with a lakeside barbecue</u>.

Wh-question: _____

Question tag type 1: _____

Question tag type 2: _____

Yes / No question: _____

47. I'm switching to a new Internet service provider <u>because I'm paying too much</u>.

Wh-question: _____

Question tag type 1: _____

Question tag type 2: _____

Yes / No question: _____

UNIT 2 | QUESTIONS IN THE PRESENT PROGRESSIVE

48. We're inviting <u>25</u> people to the reception.

Wh-question: _____

Question tag type 1: _____

Question tag type 2: _____

Yes / No question: _____

49. Nancy is talking loudly <u>to get the waiter's attention</u>.

Wh-question: _____

Question tag type 1: _____

Question tag type 2: _____

Yes / No question: _____

50. John and Markus are watching <u>a scary movie</u> on TV.

Wh-question: _____

Question tag type 1: _____

Question tag type 2: _____

Yes / No question: _____

QUESTIONS WITH MODAL VERBS:

[Note on the use of modals in American English: Of the recognized modal verbs in English, only *can*, *could*, *should*, *will*, and *would* are commonly used in spoken American English in all the question forms practiced in this book. Other modals not listed here often experience shifts in meaning, or represent forms that are now widely regarded as archaic (e.g., "shall" and "shan't"). *Must* is rarely used in positive declarative statements to express emphatic obligation and has largely been replaced by an appropriate form of "have to," or alternatively, is rephrased with *subject + is / are + required to*. Note also that the negative form (*mustn't*) becomes prohibitive; its use in tag questions is thus limited.]

51. Kathy and Suzanne could be <u>hiking</u> in the mountains.

Wh-question: _____

Question tag type 1: _____

Question tag type 2: _____

Yes / No question: _____

52. Stephen would be taking lots of snapshots if he were here.

Wh-question: _____

Question tag type 1: _____

Question tag type 2: _____

Yes / No question: _____

53. The assistant should be making the reservations.

Wh-question: _____

Question tag type 1: _____

Question tag type 2: _____

Yes / No question: _____

54. Your husband must be wearing a tie and a jacket to enter the building.

Wh-question: _____

Question tag type 1: _____

Question tag type 2: _____

Yes / No question: _____

55. You should be dancing.

Wh-question: _____

Question tag type 1: _____

Question tag type 2: _____

Yes / No question: _____

56. With our program, you can be speaking French in less than six months.

Wh-question: _____

Question tag type 1: _____

Question tag type 2: _____

Yes / No question: _____

UNIT 3

QUESTIONS IN THE PRESENT PERFECT

DIRECTIONS: Transform each of the following sentences into the type of question required in each of the given blanks. The underlined phrases in each sentence indicate which question phrase should be used.

Example:	I have drunk <u>two cups</u> of tea.
Wh-question:	How many cups of tea have you drunk?
Question tag type 1:	You've drunk two cups of tea, haven't you? [expected positive response]
Question tag type 2:	You haven't drunk two cups of tea, have you? [expected negative response]
Yes / No question:	Have you drunk two cups of tea?

1. I've seen my sister <u>twice</u> since I've been here.

Wh-question: _____

Question tag type 1: _____

Question tag type 2: _____

Yes / No question: _____

2. The kids have already eaten <u>three</u> bowls of ramen this afternoon.

Wh-question: _____

Question tag type 1: _____

Question tag type 2: _____

Yes / No question: _____

3. We've been to London more than ten times.

Wh-question: _____
Question tag type 1: _____
Question tag type 2: _____
Yes / No question: _____

4. Shayne has sent two emails to ask for more information.

Wh-question: _____
Question tag type 1: _____
Question tag type 2: _____
Yes / No question: _____

5. I've used my cell phone only twice today.

Wh-question: _____
Question tag type 1: _____
Question tag type 2: _____
Yes / No question: _____

6. They've texted us five times this week to see if we're coming to their cabin.

Wh-question: _____
Question tag type 1: _____
Question tag type 2: _____
Yes / No question: _____

7. Jean has written four books since she retired.

Wh-question: _____
Question tag type 1: _____
Question tag type 2: _____
Yes / No question: _____

UNIT 3 | QUESTIONS IN THE PRESENT PERFECT

8. We've been to Broadway theaters <u>at least 50 times</u> since we moved to New York.

Wh-question: _____

Question tag type 1: _____

Question tag type 2: _____

Yes / No question: _____

9. I've just ordered <u>a large skillet of vegetarian paella</u>.

Wh-question: _____

Question tag type 1: _____

Question tag type 2: _____

Yes / No question: _____

10. She has done professional work <u>as a computer systems analyst</u>.

Wh-question: _____

Question tag type 1: _____

Question tag type 2: _____

Yes / No question: _____

11. I have taken <u>some</u> of the medicine.

Wh-question: _____

Question tag type 1: _____

Question tag type 2: _____

Yes / No question: _____

12. John has played <u>four</u> different instruments since he started studying music.

Wh-question: _____

Question tag type 1: _____

Question tag type 2: _____

Yes / No question: _____

13. Marcia has been a landscape architect <u>for 20 years</u>.

Wh-question: _____

Question tag type 1: _____

Question tag type 2: _____

Yes / No question: _____

14. <u>Woo-Young</u> has booked the hotel rooms in San Francisco.

Wh-question: _____

Question tag type 1: _____

Question tag type 2: _____

Yes / No question: _____

15. <u>Our marketing department</u> has contacted company headquarters in Japan.

Wh-question: _____

Question tag type 1: _____

Question tag type 2: _____

Yes / No question: _____

16. The software company has just opened its new training center <u>in Mumbai</u>.

Wh-question: _____

Question tag type 1: _____

Question tag type 2: _____

Yes / No question: _____

17. We have reserved <u>500</u> chairs for the conference.

Wh-question: _____

Question tag type 1: _____

Question tag type 2: _____

Yes / No question: _____

UNIT 3 | QUESTIONS IN THE PRESENT PERFECT

18. <u>The chair of our department</u> has just received the Nobel Prize in chemistry.

Wh-question: _____

Question tag type 1: _____

Question tag type 2: _____

Yes / No question: _____

19. I've taken <u>four</u> exams this week.

Wh-question: _____

Question tag type 1: _____

Question tag type 2: _____

Yes / No question: _____

20. Daniel has received a job offer <u>from Google</u>.

Wh-question: _____

Question tag type 1: _____

Question tag type 2: _____

Yes / No question: _____

21. My wife and I have visited <u>65</u> countries.

Wh-question: _____

Question tag type 1: _____

Question tag type 2: _____

Yes / No question: _____

22. My grandmother has been <u>quite well</u> recently.

Wh-question: _____

Question tag type 1: _____

Question tag type 2: _____

Yes / No question: _____

23. I've complained to the landlord about the deafening music next door.

Wh-question: _____

Question tag type 1: _____

Question tag type 2: _____

Yes / No question: _____

24. Dorothy has cooked enough food for 10 people.

Wh-question: _____

Question tag type 1: _____

Question tag type 2: _____

Yes / No question: _____

25. Erin has spoken to her parents and to the school counselor about her aggressive French teacher.

Wh-question: _____

Question tag type 1: _____

Question tag type 2: _____

Yes / No question: _____

26. Matthew has been in the hospital for the last three days.

Wh-question: _____

Question tag type 1: _____

Question tag type 2: _____

Yes / No question: _____

27. Matthew has been in the hospital for the last three days.

Wh-question: _____

Question tag type 1: _____

Question tag type 2: _____

Yes / No question: _____

UNIT 3 | QUESTIONS IN THE PRESENT PERFECT

28. Naomi has seen her family <u>twice</u> this year.

Wh-question: _____

Question tag type 1: _____

Question tag type 2: _____

Yes / No question: _____

29. Timothy has fed the fish <u>twice</u> today.

Wh-question: _____

Question tag type 1: _____

Question tag type 2: _____

Yes / No question: _____

30. I've flown across the Pacific <u>five times</u>.

Wh-question: _____

Question tag type 1: _____

Question tag type 2: _____

Yes / No question: _____

31. My sister-in-law has written <u>seven</u> books.

Wh-question: _____

Question tag type 1: _____

Question tag type 2: _____

Yes / No question: _____

32. Daoud has been to Mecca <u>more than 10 times</u>.

Wh-question: _____

Question tag type 1: _____

Question tag type 2: _____

Yes / No question: _____

33. Martina has opened three bottles of red wine.

Wh-question: _____
Question tag type 1: _____
Question tag type 2: _____
Yes / No question: _____

34. Karsten has just bought a new Lamborghini sports car.

Wh-question: _____
Question tag type 1: _____
Question tag type 2: _____
Yes / No question: _____

35. Sarah has gone to the Himalayas on vacation.

Wh-question: _____
Question tag type 1: _____
Question tag type 2: _____
Yes / No question: _____

36. My uncle has met five presidents of the United States.

Wh-question: _____
Question tag type 1: _____
Question tag type 2: _____
Yes / No question: _____

37. Claudia has been a judge for more than 15 years.

Wh-question: _____
Question tag type 1: _____
Question tag type 2: _____
Yes / No question: _____

UNIT 3 | QUESTIONS IN THE PRESENT PERFECT

38. Jason has become the new CEO of our company.

Wh-question: _____
Question tag type 1: _____
Question tag type 2: _____
Yes / No question: _____

39. Robert has placed the order for refreshments.

Wh-question: _____
Question tag type 1: _____
Question tag type 2: _____
Yes / No question: _____

40. Our neighbors have painted their kitchen yellow.

Wh-question: _____
Question tag type 1: _____
Question tag type 2: _____
Yes / No question: _____

41. Our neighbors have painted their kitchen yellow.

Wh-question: _____
Question tag type 1: _____
Question tag type 2: _____
Yes / No question: _____

42. A businessman from Moscow has bought the 10-carat red diamond.

Wh-question: _____
Question tag type 1: _____
Question tag type 2: _____
Yes / No question: _____

43. The company has conducted <u>35</u> test flights in the new airplane.

Wh-question: _____

Question tag type 1: _____

Question tag type 2: _____

Yes / No question: _____

44. I have waited <u>for six months</u> to see this play.

Wh-question: _____

Question tag type 1: _____

Question tag type 2: _____

Yes / No question: _____

45. The UK has had <u>only one</u> prime minister named "Thatcher."

Wh-question: _____

Question tag type 1: _____

Question tag type 2: _____

Yes / No question: _____

46. I've gone through <u>four</u> pairs of shoes in just the last year.

Wh-question: _____

Question tag type 1: _____

Question tag type 2: _____

Yes / No question: _____

47. We've walked <u>more than six miles</u> since this morning.

Wh-question: _____

Question tag type 1: _____

Question tag type 2: _____

Yes / No question: _____

UNIT 3 | QUESTIONS IN THE PRESENT PERFECT   37

48. I've sold <u>the old tripod</u> at our garage sale.

Wh-question: _____

Question tag type 1: _____

Question tag type 2: _____

Yes / No question: _____

49. This chair has been in our family <u>for over 100 years</u>.

Wh-question: _____

Question tag type 1: _____

Question tag type 2: _____

Yes / No question: _____

50. The Hensons have taken their children <u>to the lake</u>.

Wh-question: _____

Question tag type 1: _____

Question tag type 2: _____

Yes / No question: _____

QUESTIONS WITH MODAL VERBS:

[Note on the use of modals in American English: Of the recognized modal verbs in English, only *can*, *could*, *should*, *will*, and *would* are commonly used in spoken American English in all the question forms practiced in this book. Other modals not listed here often experience shifts in meaning, or represent forms that are now widely regarded as archaic (e.g., "shall" and "shan't"). Must is rarely used in positive declarative statements to express emphatic obligation and has largely been replaced by an appropriate form of "have to," or alternatively, is rephrased with subject + is / are + required to. Note also that the negative form (mustn't) becomes prohibitive; its use in tag questions is thus limited.]

51. <u>Po-Yi</u> should have reported the theft to the police.

Wh-question: _____

Question tag type 1: _____

Question tag type 2: _____

Yes / No question: _____

52. Sara could have gone to work <u>by taxi</u>.

Wh-question: _____
Question tag type 1: _____
Question tag type 2: _____
Yes / No question: _____

53. <u>Vladimir</u> might have won the chess tournament.

Wh-question: _____
Question tag type 1: _____
Question tag type 2: _____
Yes / No question: _____

54. Jane would have <u>screamed</u>.

Wh-question: _____
Question tag type 1: _____
Question tag type 2: _____
Yes / No question: _____

55. The company should have contacted <u>the ministry of trade</u>.

Wh-question: _____
Question tag type 1: _____
Question tag type 2: _____
Yes / No question: _____

56. <u>Tom</u> should have disclosed this information.

Wh-question: _____
Question tag type 1: _____
Question tag type 2: _____
Yes / No question: _____

UNIT 4

QUESTIONS IN THE PRESENT PERFECT PROGRESSIVE

DIRECTIONS: Transform each of the following sentences into the type of question required in each of the given blanks. The underlined phrases in each sentence indicate which question phrase should be used.

Example:	*Glenda has been <u>reading</u>.*
Wh-question:	*What has Glenda been doing?*
Question tag type 1:	*Glenda has been reading, hasn't she?* [expected positive response]
Question tag type 2:	*Glenda hasn't been reading, has she?* [expected negative response]
Yes / No question:	*Has Glenda been reading?*

1. Our team has been studying English <u>for the last five years</u>.

Wh-question: _____

Question tag type 1: _____

Question tag type 2: _____

Yes / No question: _____

2. We have been living <u>in Oman</u> for the last 10 years.

Wh-question: _____

Question tag type 1: _____

Question tag type 2: _____

Yes / No question: _____

3. I have been working at HAL since 2007.

Wh-question: _____

Question tag type 1: _____

Question tag type 2: _____

Yes / No question: _____

4. Richard has been writing for more than three hours.

Wh-question: _____

Question tag type 1: _____

Question tag type 2: _____

Yes / No question: _____

5. I have been traveling and working as a photojournalist since we last spoke.

Wh-question: _____

Question tag type 1: _____

Question tag type 2: _____

Yes / No question: _____

6. Carla has been eating the chocolate cookies.

Wh-question: _____

Question tag type 1: _____

Question tag type 2: _____

Yes / No question: _____

7. Carla has been eating the chocolate cookies.

Wh-question: _____

Question tag type 1: _____

Question tag type 2: _____

Yes / No question: _____

8. Chris has been skiing in the Rocky Mountains.

Wh-question: _____
Question tag type 1: _____
Question tag type 2: _____
Yes / No question: _____

9. Chris has been skiing in the Rocky Mountains.

Wh-question: _____
Question tag type 1: _____
Question tag type 2: _____
Yes / No question: _____

10. The baby has been sleeping since two this afternoon.

Wh-question: _____
Question tag type 1: _____
Question tag type 2: _____
Yes / No question: _____

11. We've been driving since 8:00 this morning.

Wh-question: _____
Question tag type 1: _____
Question tag type 2: _____
Yes / No question: _____

12. The baby's been sleeping all afternoon.

Wh-question: _____
Question tag type 1: _____
Question tag type 2: _____
Yes / No question: _____

13. We've been <u>driving</u> all morning.

Wh-question: _____

Question tag type 1: _____

Question tag type 2: _____

Yes / No question: _____

14. <u>The neighbors downstairs</u> have been making all the noise.

Wh-question: _____

Question tag type 1: _____

Question tag type 2: _____

Yes / No question: _____

15. The neighbors downstairs have been <u>barbecuing in the driveway</u>.

Wh-question: _____

Question tag type 1: _____

Question tag type 2: _____

Yes / No question: _____

16. <u>My nephew</u> has been doing the gardening at our house.

Wh-question: _____

Question tag type 1: _____

Question tag type 2: _____

Yes / No question: _____

17. Janet and her husband have been reducing their debt <u>by spending less each month</u>.

Wh-question: _____

Question tag type 1: _____

Question tag type 2: _____

Yes / No question: _____

UNIT 4 | QUESTIONS IN THE PRESENT PERFECT PROGRESSIVE

18. Jan has been improving his English skills <u>by going to evening classes</u>.

Wh-question: _____
Question tag type 1: _____
Question tag type 2: _____
Yes / No question: _____

19. Our company has been expanding <u>by opening up branches in Asia</u>.

Wh-question: _____
Question tag type 1: _____
Question tag type 2: _____
Yes / No question: _____

20. Heather has been working <u>over 50 hours per week</u> for the last four months.

Wh-question: _____
Question tag type 1: _____
Question tag type 2: _____
Yes / No question: _____

21. We've been paying <u>over $1,000 per week</u> for this leased car.

Wh-question: _____
Question tag type 1: _____
Question tag type 2: _____
Yes / No question: _____

22. I have recently been swimming <u>every morning for two hours</u>.

Wh-question: _____
Question tag type 1: _____
Question tag type 2: _____
Yes / No question: _____

23. Teresa has been working overtime to improve her income.

Wh-question: _____
Question tag type 1: _____
Question tag type 2: _____
Yes / No question: _____

24. The Finnish National Symphony has been performing in Melbourne and Sydney this week.

Wh-question: _____
Question tag type 1: _____
Question tag type 2: _____
Yes / No question: _____

25. John has been chewing gum to help him break his smoking addiction.

Wh-question: _____
Question tag type 1: _____
Question tag type 2: _____
Yes / No question: _____

26. I've been feeling quite good the last several weeks.

Wh-question: _____
Question tag type 1: _____
Question tag type 2: _____
Yes / No question: _____

27. The company has been delivering our supplies every Tuesday and Friday.

Wh-question: _____
Question tag type 1: _____
Question tag type 2: _____
Yes / No question: _____

UNIT 4 | QUESTIONS IN THE PRESENT PERFECT PROGRESSIVE

28. Monica has been playing tennis <u>since she was five years old</u>.

Wh-question: _____
Question tag type 1: _____
Question tag type 2: _____
Yes / No question: _____

29. I have been <u>working on my new book</u> since we last saw each other.

Wh-question: _____
Question tag type 1: _____
Question tag type 2: _____
Yes / No question: _____

30. Our daughter has been studying <u>chemistry</u> at Johns Hopkins University.

Wh-question: _____
Question tag type 1: _____
Question tag type 2: _____
Yes / No question: _____

31. Our son has been studying conducting <u>at the Curtis Institute</u>.

Wh-question: _____
Question tag type 1: _____
Question tag type 2: _____
Yes / No question: _____

32. My closest friend has been living <u>in the Knightsbridge area</u> of London.

Wh-question: _____
Question tag type 1: _____
Question tag type 2: _____
Yes / No question: _____

33. We have been making <u>vegetarian dumplings</u>.

Wh-question: _____

Question tag type 1: _____

Question tag type 2: _____

Yes / No question: _____

34. <u>George</u> has been washing the dishes.

Wh-question: _____

Question tag type 1: _____

Question tag type 2: _____

Yes / No question: _____

35. Andrea has been <u>washing the clothes</u> in the basement.

Wh-question: _____

Question tag type 1: _____

Question tag type 2: _____

Yes / No question: _____

36. Andrea has been washing the clothes <u>in the basement</u>.

Wh-question: _____

Question tag type 1: _____

Question tag type 2: _____

Yes / No question: _____

37. ITCD has been building <u>new learning centers</u> this year.

Wh-question: _____

Question tag type 1: _____

Question tag type 2: _____

Yes / No question: _____

UNIT 4 | QUESTIONS IN THE PRESENT PERFECT PROGRESSIVE

38. The committee has been raising concerns about the legality of these transactions.

Wh-question: _____
Question tag type 1: _____
Question tag type 2: _____
Yes / No question: _____

39. The meteorological institute has been using sophisticated software to map the storm's path.

Wh-question: _____
Question tag type 1: _____
Question tag type 2: _____
Yes / No question: _____

40. The kids have been hiding in plain sight the whole time.

Wh-question: _____
Question tag type 1: _____
Question tag type 2: _____
Yes / No question: _____

41. Pat has been texting for more than two hours.

Wh-question: _____
Question tag type 1: _____
Question tag type 2: _____
Yes / No question: _____

42. The central banks have been manipulating the price of gold and silver.

Wh-question: _____
Question tag type 1: _____
Question tag type 2: _____
Yes / No question: _____

43. Shijie has been traveling to New York twice a month.

Wh-question: _____

Question tag type 1: _____

Question tag type 2: _____

Yes / No question: _____

44. I've been talking to the manager about the broken faucets in the bathroom.

Wh-question: _____

Question tag type 1: _____

Question tag type 2: _____

Yes / No question: _____

45. My brother has been dancing the night away tonight on the west side of town.

Wh-question: _____

Question tag type 1: _____

Question tag type 2: _____

Yes / No question: _____

46. The fuel sensor has been causing the problems in her car.

Wh-question: _____

Question tag type 1: _____

Question tag type 2: _____

Yes / No question: _____

47. The last job applicant has been calling all morning long.

Wh-question: _____

Question tag type 1: _____

Question tag type 2: _____

Yes / No question: _____

UNIT 4 | QUESTIONS IN THE PRESENT PERFECT PROGRESSIVE

48. The university has been using <u>an all-natural product</u> to clean the floors.

Wh-question: _____

Question tag type 1: _____

Question tag type 2: _____

Yes / No question: _____

49. Suzanne has been getting her hair cut <u>at a salon in Chelsea</u>.

Wh-question: _____

Question tag type 1: _____

Question tag type 2: _____

Yes / No question: _____

50. Evelyn and Mark have been spending their honeymoon <u>in the Bahamas</u>.

Wh-question: _____

Question tag type 1: _____

Question tag type 2: _____

Yes / No question: _____

QUESTIONS WITH MODAL VERBS:

[Note on the use of modals in American English: Of the recognized modal verbs in English, only *can*, *could*, *should*, *will*, and *would* are commonly used in spoken American English in all the question forms practiced in this book. Other modals not listed here often experience shifts in meaning, or represent forms that are now widely regarded as archaic (e.g., "shall" and "shan't"). *Must* is rarely used in positive declarative statements to express emphatic obligation and has largely been replaced by an appropriate form of "have to," or alternatively, is rephrased with *subject + is / are + required to*. Note also that the negative form (*mustn't*) becomes prohibitive; its use in tag questions is thus limited.]

51. Jason should have been driving <u>under 40 km per hour</u>.

Wh-question: _____

Question tag type 1: _____

Question tag type 2: _____

Yes / No question: _____

52. Maria could have been <u>cooking dinner</u>.

Wh-question: _____
Question tag type 1: _____
Question tag type 2: _____
Yes / No question: _____

53. Sam might have been <u>sleeping</u> at the time of the robbery.

Wh-question: _____
Question tag type 1: _____
Question tag type 2: _____
Yes / No question: _____

54. Grace could have been <u>listening to music</u> during the storm.

Wh-question: _____
Question tag type 1: _____
Question tag type 2: _____
Yes / No question: _____

55. <u>A train</u> might have been making that awful noise last night.

Wh-question: _____
Question tag type 1: _____
Question tag type 2: _____
Yes / No question: _____

56. Rachel's son should have been doing <u>his homework</u> this evening.

Wh-question: _____
Question tag type 1: _____
Question tag type 2: _____
Yes / No question: _____

UNIT 5

QUESTIONS IN THE PAST SIMPLE

DIRECTIONS: Transform each of the following sentences into the type of question required in each of the given blanks. The underlined phrases in each sentence indicate which question phrase should be used.

Example:	*Janice ate the cake.*
Wh-question:	*What did Janice eat?*
Question tag type 1:	*Janice ate the cake, didn't she?* [expected positive response]
Question tag type 2:	*Janice didn't eat the cake, did she?* [expected negative response]
Yes / No question:	*Did Janice eat the cake?*

1. Shakespeare wrote *Macbeth*.

Wh-question: _____

Question tag type 1: _____

Question tag type 2: _____

Yes / No question: _____

2. I called the office at around 9 p.m.

Wh-question: _____

Question tag type 1: _____

Question tag type 2: _____

Yes / No question: _____

3. Sheila made vegetarian risotto for dinner last night.

Wh-question: _____

Question tag type 1: _____

Question tag type 2: _____

Yes / No question: _____

4. We went to Ireland on vacation last year.

Wh-question: _____

Question tag type 1: _____

Question tag type 2: _____

Yes / No question: _____

5. He traveled by boat from San Juan to Curaçao.

Wh-question: _____

Question tag type 1: _____

Question tag type 2: _____

Yes / No question: _____

6. He apologized at least 10 times for forgetting my birthday.

Wh-question: _____

Question tag type 1: _____

Question tag type 2: _____

Yes / No question: _____

7. We played tennis every afternoon on our trip to Spain.

Wh-question: _____

Question tag type 1: _____

Question tag type 2: _____

Yes / No question: _____

8. We saw <u>Helen Mirren</u> in Beverly Hills.

Wh-question: _____

Question tag type 1: _____

Question tag type 2: _____

Yes / No question: _____

9. I voted for <u>a Green Party candidate</u> in the last election.

Wh-question: _____

Question tag type 1: _____

Question tag type 2: _____

Yes / No question: _____

10. I played <u>the violin</u> in the university orchestra.

Wh-question: _____

Question tag type 1: _____

Question tag type 2: _____

Yes / No question: _____

11. I was <u>15</u> when I learned to drive.

Wh-question: _____

Question tag type 1: _____

Question tag type 2: _____

Yes / No question: _____

12. My mother bought that sweater <u>in Donegal, Ireland</u>.

Wh-question: _____

Question tag type 1: _____

Question tag type 2: _____

Yes / No question: _____

13. We lived in London when I was a child.

Wh-question: _____
Question tag type 1: _____
Question tag type 2: _____
Yes / No question: _____

14. I dreamed about my calculus exam last night.

Wh-question: _____
Question tag type 1: _____
Question tag type 2: _____
Yes / No question: _____

15. I went to work by subway this morning.

Wh-question: _____
Question tag type 1: _____
Question tag type 2: _____
Yes / No question: _____

16. My sister graduated last month.

Wh-question: _____
Question tag type 1: _____
Question tag type 2: _____
Yes / No question: _____

17. A storm caused this damage to the roof.

Wh-question: _____
Question tag type 1: _____
Question tag type 2: _____
Yes / No question: _____

UNIT 5 | QUESTIONS IN THE PAST SIMPLE

18. My parents paid <u>more than $500</u> for their dinner in Rome.

Wh-question: _____

Question tag type 1: _____

Question tag type 2: _____

Yes / No question: _____

19. We lost <u>over $2,000</u> in Las Vegas.

Wh-question: _____

Question tag type 1: _____

Question tag type 2: _____

Yes / No question: _____

20. <u>Carla's little boy</u> broke the iPad.

Wh-question: _____

Question tag type 1: _____

Question tag type 2: _____

Yes / No question: _____

21. My uncle broke his leg <u>last December</u>.

Wh-question: _____

Question tag type 1: _____

Question tag type 2: _____

Yes / No question: _____

22. Caroline and David named their new daughter "<u>Marguerite</u>."

Wh-question: _____

Question tag type 1: _____

Question tag type 2: _____

Yes / No question: _____

23. I fed the dog at 10 this morning.

Wh-question: _____
Question tag type 1: _____
Question tag type 2: _____
Yes / No question: _____

24. Bruce saw a bank robbery yesterday.

Wh-question: _____
Question tag type 1: _____
Question tag type 2: _____
Yes / No question: _____

25. I woke up at 6:30 this morning.

Wh-question: _____
Question tag type 1: _____
Question tag type 2: _____
Yes / No question: _____

26. We went to bed at 12:30 last night.

Wh-question: _____
Question tag type 1: _____
Question tag type 2: _____
Yes / No question: _____

27. Ramesh quit his job at the software company to start his own business.

Wh-question: _____
Question tag type 1: _____
Question tag type 2: _____
Yes / No question: _____

UNIT 5 | QUESTIONS IN THE PAST SIMPLE

28. Sara screamed because of the intruder.

Wh-question: _____
Question tag type 1: _____
Question tag type 2: _____
Yes / No question: _____

29. We read Tolstoy's *War and Peace* in our literature class.

Wh-question: _____
Question tag type 1: _____
Question tag type 2: _____
Yes / No question: _____

30. We painted our living room red.

Wh-question: _____
Question tag type 1: _____
Question tag type 2: _____
Yes / No question: _____

31. Kathy bought a two-door sports car.

Wh-question: _____
Question tag type 1: _____
Question tag type 2: _____
Yes / No question: _____

32. Jeff bought his girlfriend a tennis bracelet for her birthday.

Wh-question: _____
Question tag type 1: _____
Question tag type 2: _____
Yes / No question: _____

33. Bob and Alice went to the Canary Islands for spring break.

Wh-question: _____

Question tag type 1: _____

Question tag type 2: _____

Yes / No question: _____

34. The class went surfing on the north shore of Oahu.

Wh-question: _____

Question tag type 1: _____

Question tag type 2: _____

Yes / No question: _____

35. Toshi ate six pancakes for breakfast this morning.

Wh-question: _____

Question tag type 1: _____

Question tag type 2: _____

Yes / No question: _____

36. The office charged me $50 for the new key.

Wh-question: _____

Question tag type 1: _____

Question tag type 2: _____

Yes / No question: _____

37. Omar grew up in Egypt.

Wh-question: _____

Question tag type 1: _____

Question tag type 2: _____

Yes / No question: _____

UNIT 5 | QUESTIONS IN THE PAST SIMPLE

38. I slept only four hours last night.

Wh-question: _____

Question tag type 1: _____

Question tag type 2: _____

Yes / No question: _____

39. Diane was at Juilliard for three years.

Wh-question: _____

Question tag type 1: _____

Question tag type 2: _____

Yes / No question: _____

40. Christine tore her pants on a piece of metal.

Wh-question: _____

Question tag type 1: _____

Question tag type 2: _____

Yes / No question: _____

41. Susan had her third child in 2013.

Wh-question: _____

Question tag type 1: _____

Question tag type 2: _____

Yes / No question: _____

42. Paula took the Air France flight to Dubai.

Wh-question: _____

Question tag type 1: _____

Question tag type 2: _____

Yes / No question: _____

43. We left for work at 8:15.

Wh-question: _____

Question tag type 1: _____

Question tag type 2: _____

Yes / No question: _____

44. Sandra bought the scarf in Venice.

Wh-question: _____

Question tag type 1: _____

Question tag type 2: _____

Yes / No question: _____

45. The food at the party yesterday was delicious.

Wh-question: _____

Question tag type 1: _____

Question tag type 2: _____

Yes / No question: _____

46. Karl drank beer with his lunch.

Wh-question: _____

Question tag type 1: _____

Question tag type 2: _____

Yes / No question: _____

47. My parents spoke both Mandarin and Cantonese at home.

Wh-question: _____

Question tag type 1: _____

Question tag type 2: _____

Yes / No question: _____

UNIT 5 | QUESTIONS IN THE PAST SIMPLE

48. I thought the movie was <u>terrible</u>.

Wh-question: _____

Question tag type 1: _____

Question tag type 2: _____

Yes / No question: _____

49. We heard <u>someone whispering</u> when we opened the door.

Wh-question: _____

Question tag type 1: _____

Question tag type 2: _____

Yes / No question: _____

50. We spent the night <u>in Sequoia National Park</u>.

Wh-question: _____

Question tag type 1: _____

Question tag type 2: _____

Yes / No question: _____

UNIT 6

QUESTIONS IN THE PAST PROGRESSIVE

DIRECTIONS: Transform each of the following sentences into the type of question required in each of the given blanks. The underlined phrases in each sentence indicate which question phrase should be used.

Example:	*Luca was having dinner <u>at the Korean restaurant</u> when his mother called.*
Wh-question:	*Where was Luca having dinner when his mother called?*
Question tag type 1:	*Luca was having dinner at the Korean restaurant when his mother called, wasn't he?* [expected positive response]
Question tag type 2:	*Luca wasn't having dinner at the Korean restaurant when his mother called, was he?* [expected negative response]
Yes / No question:	*Was Luca having dinner at the Korean restaurant when his mother called?*

1. Tetsuya was sleeping <u>on the couch</u> when the burglar broke in.

Wh-question: _____

Question tag type 1: _____

Question tag type 2: _____

Yes / No question: _____

UNIT 6 | QUESTIONS IN THE PAST PROGRESSIVE 63

2. We were <u>eating dinner in the dining room</u> when we heard the crash.

Wh-question: _____

Question tag type 1: _____

Question tag type 2: _____

Yes / No question: _____

3. I was <u>uploading videos</u> when the computer crashed.

Wh-question: _____

Question tag type 1: _____

Question tag type 2: _____

Yes / No question: _____

4. Isaac was <u>bowling with his friends</u> when he lost his keys.

Wh-question: _____

Question tag type 1: _____

Question tag type 2: _____

Yes / No question: _____

5. I was talking <u>to my fiancé</u> when you ran into me on the street.

Wh-question: _____

Question tag type 1: _____

Question tag type 2: _____

Yes / No question: _____

6. We were going <u>to an art exhibit</u> when we got robbed.

Wh-question: _____

Question tag type 1: _____

Question tag type 2: _____

Yes / No question: _____

7. Simon was paying $2,000 for his studio apartment during his year in San Francisco.

Wh-question: _____

Question tag type 1: _____

Question tag type 2: _____

Yes / No question: _____

8. We were living in Hawaii when we met.

Wh-question: _____

Question tag type 1: _____

Question tag type 2: _____

Yes / No question: _____

9. Kees was carrying four suitcases when he fell.

Wh-question: _____

Question tag type 1: _____

Question tag type 2: _____

Yes / No question: _____

10. Frank was talking to Martha when he got the text message from his brother.

Wh-question: _____

Question tag type 1: _____

Question tag type 2: _____

Yes / No question: _____

11. I was feeling ill when I got out of bed this morning.

Wh-question: _____

Question tag type 1: _____

Question tag type 2: _____

Yes / No question: _____

12. <u>Mark</u> was working at the computer when the monitor caught fire.

Wh-question: _____
Question tag type 1: _____
Question tag type 2: _____
Yes / No question: _____

13. My parents were talking <u>about their summer vacation</u> during dinner.

Wh-question: _____
Question tag type 1: _____
Question tag type 2: _____
Yes / No question: _____

14. We were going <u>to Joshua Tree Forest</u> when our front tire blew out.

Wh-question: _____
Question tag type 1: _____
Question tag type 2: _____
Yes / No question: _____

15. I was talking <u>to my boss</u> when I heard the sirens.

Wh-question: _____
Question tag type 1: _____
Question tag type 2: _____
Yes / No question: _____

16. We were just <u>boarding up the windows</u> when the hurricane hit.

Wh-question: _____
Question tag type 1: _____
Question tag type 2: _____
Yes / No question: _____

17. Thomas was living in Chicago when he first took up the bassoon.

Wh-question: _____
Question tag type 1: _____
Question tag type 2: _____
Yes / No question: _____

18. We were treating more than 100 patients a week during our first month on duty.

Wh-question: _____
Question tag type 1: _____
Question tag type 2: _____
Yes / No question: _____

19. Jessie was swimming in the pool when her labor pains started.

Wh-question: _____
Question tag type 1: _____
Question tag type 2: _____
Yes / No question: _____

20. I was having breakfast with three classmates when you saw me.

Wh-question: _____
Question tag type 1: _____
Question tag type 2: _____
Yes / No question: _____

21. My husband was studying physics when we first met.

Wh-question: _____
Question tag type 1: _____
Question tag type 2: _____
Yes / No question: _____

UNIT 6 | QUESTIONS IN THE PAST PROGRESSIVE   67

22. We were <u>taking pictures of the sunset</u> when we saw the strange lights in the sky.

Wh-question: _____

Question tag type 1: _____

Question tag type 2: _____

Yes / No question: _____

23. Samantha was listening to <u>an old song by Michael Jackson</u> when she started crying.

Wh-question: _____

Question tag type 1: _____

Question tag type 2: _____

Yes / No question: _____

24. My aunt was <u>talking to her lawyer</u> when the judge told her to be quiet.

Wh-question: _____

Question tag type 1: _____

Question tag type 2: _____

Yes / No question: _____

25. Maria was singing <u>movie theme songs</u> when everyone started clapping.

Wh-question: _____

Question tag type 1: _____

Question tag type 2: _____

Yes / No question: _____

26. John and Claudine were working <u>in Silicon Valley</u> when they met each other.

Wh-question: _____

Question tag type 1: _____

Question tag type 2: _____

Yes / No question: _____

27. <u>Dorothy</u> was taking care of the cat while Lucienne was away on vacation.

Wh-question: _____

Question tag type 1: _____

Question tag type 2: _____

Yes / No question: _____

28. Michael was sleeping <u>in the guest room</u> while the repair work was going on.

Wh-question: _____

Question tag type 1: _____

Question tag type 2: _____

Yes / No question: _____

29. Shao-yen was teaching <u>at Oxford</u> from 2011 through 2013.

Wh-question: _____

Question tag type 1: _____

Question tag type 2: _____

Yes / No question: _____

30. Shirley was living in Rome <u>from 2002 through 2009</u>.

Wh-question: _____

Question tag type 1: _____

Question tag type 2: _____

Yes / No question: _____

31. Mike was skiing <u>in Colorado</u> when he fell and broke his arm.

Wh-question: _____

Question tag type 1: _____

Question tag type 2: _____

Yes / No question: _____

UNIT 6 | QUESTIONS IN THE PAST PROGRESSIVE   69

32. I was standing <u>on a chair</u> when I suddenly felt dizzy.

Wh-question: _____

Question tag type 1: _____

Question tag type 2: _____

Yes / No question: _____

33. Alan was carrying <u>dangerous chemicals</u> when he tripped and fell.

Wh-question: _____

Question tag type 1: _____

Question tag type 2: _____

Yes / No question: _____

34. <u>Our neighbors</u> were taking care of our garden while we were gone.

Wh-question: _____

Question tag type 1: _____

Question tag type 2: _____

Yes / No question: _____

35. <u>Mr. Johnson</u> was yelling at the employees at closing time.

Wh-question: _____

Question tag type 1: _____

Question tag type 2: _____

Yes / No question: _____

36. We were going <u>75 km/h</u> when the brakes failed.

Wh-question: _____

Question tag type 1: _____

Question tag type 2: _____

Yes / No question: _____

37. I was watching <u>a soccer match</u> on TV when the power went out.

Wh-question: _____

Question tag type 1: _____

Question tag type 2: _____

Yes / No question: _____

38. I was <u>playing computer games</u> when lightning struck the tree.

Wh-question: _____

Question tag type 1: _____

Question tag type 2: _____

Yes / No question: _____

39. Jeffrey was arguing <u>with his office mate</u> when the director came in.

Wh-question: _____

Question tag type 1: _____

Question tag type 2: _____

Yes / No question: _____

40. We were <u>watching an online video</u> when the professor entered the classroom.

Wh-question: _____

Question tag type 1: _____

Question tag type 2: _____

Yes / No question: _____

41. During the heat wave last summer, I was taking a shower <u>twice a day</u>.

Wh-question: _____

Question tag type 1: _____

Question tag type 2: _____

Yes / No question: _____

UNIT 6 | QUESTIONS IN THE PAST PROGRESSIVE

42. Before I tore the tendon in my foot, I was swimming <u>every day</u>.

Wh-question: _____

Question tag type 1: _____

Question tag type 2: _____

Yes / No question: _____

43. I was eating <u>popcorn</u> when the fly flew into my mouth.

Wh-question: _____

Question tag type 1: _____

Question tag type 2: _____

Yes / No question: _____

44. Caroline was talking <u>to her father</u> on the phone when the bee stung her.

Wh-question: _____

Question tag type 1: _____

Question tag type 2: _____

Yes / No question: _____

45. I was texting <u>my professor</u> when my phone froze up.

Wh-question: _____

Question tag type 1: _____

Question tag type 2: _____

Yes / No question: _____

46. Bob was <u>taking a bath</u> when the alarm went off.

Wh-question: _____

Question tag type 1: _____

Question tag type 2: _____

Yes / No question: _____

47. I was driving 50 km/h when the police stopped me.

Wh-question: _____

Question tag type 1: _____

Question tag type 2: _____

Yes / No question: _____

48. I was sitting in a rear aisle seat during the flight.

Wh-question: _____

Question tag type 1: _____

Question tag type 2: _____

Yes / No question: _____

49. My wife was walking to work during the first six months after the earthquake.

Wh-question: _____

Question tag type 1: _____

Question tag type 2: _____

Yes / No question: _____

50. We were feeding the baby puréed vegetables when she began to cry.

Wh-question: _____

Question tag type 1: _____

Question tag type 2: _____

Yes / No question: _____

UNIT 7

QUESTIONS IN THE PAST PERFECT

DIRECTIONS: Transform each of the following sentences into the type of question required in each of the given blanks. The underlined phrases in each sentence indicate which question phrase should be used.

Example:	*By 9 a.m., Fernando had already drunk <u>10</u> cups of coffee.*
Wh-question:	*How many cups of coffee had Fernando already drunk by 9 a.m.?*
Question tag type 1:	*Fernando had already drunk 10 cups of coffee by 9 a.m., hadn't he?* [expected positive response]
Question tag type 2:	*Fernando hadn't already drunk 10 cups of coffee by 9 a.m., had he?* [expected negative response]
Yes / No question:	*Had Fernando already drunk 10 cups of coffee by 9 a.m.?*

1. Antonio had already seen the film <u>four times</u> before it opened in the cinemas.

Wh-question: _____

Question tag type 1: _____

Question tag type 2: _____

Yes / No question: _____

2. We had been at the station for <u>more than three hours</u> before you arrived.

Wh-question: _____
Question tag type 1: _____
Question tag type 2: _____
Yes / No question: _____

3. The company directors had interviewed <u>80</u> applicants before making their decision.

Wh-question: _____
Question tag type 1: _____
Question tag type 2: _____
Yes / No question: _____

4. Georgina had been sick <u>for two days</u> before she went to the doctor.

Wh-question: _____
Question tag type 1: _____
Question tag type 2: _____
Yes / No question: _____

5. The employees had worked <u>for three months</u> before they ever saw their first salary.

Wh-question: _____
Question tag type 1: _____
Question tag type 2: _____
Yes / No question: _____

6. We had eaten <u>most of the food</u> when we learned it wasn't for us.

Wh-question: _____
Question tag type 1: _____
Question tag type 2: _____
Yes / No question: _____

UNIT 7 | QUESTIONS IN THE PAST PERFECT

7. My cousins had been <u>in Rome</u> before they traveled to Paris.

Wh-question: _____

Question tag type 1: _____

Question tag type 2: _____

Yes / No question: _____

8. Martino had played the piano <u>for three years</u> before he took up the guitar.

Wh-question: _____

Question tag type 1: _____

Question tag type 2: _____

Yes / No question: _____

9. I had studied Russian <u>for two years</u> before I began Arabic.

Wh-question: _____

Question tag type 1: _____

Question tag type 2: _____

Yes / No question: _____

10. I had been <u>in town</u> before you dropped by.

Wh-question: _____

Question tag type 1: _____

Question tag type 2: _____

Yes / No question: _____

11. By the time James finished preparing breakfast, he had eaten <u>six</u> of the pancakes.

Wh-question: _____

Question tag type 1: _____

Question tag type 2: _____

Yes / No question: _____

12. Tanya had lived in <u>five</u> countries by the time she was 12.

Wh-question: _____

Question tag type 1: _____

Question tag type 2: _____

Yes / No question: _____

13. My aunt had called the police <u>four times</u> before they responded.

Wh-question: _____

Question tag type 1: _____

Question tag type 2: _____

Yes / No question: _____

14. <u>Carol</u> had bolted down the windows before the storm blew in.

Wh-question: _____

Question tag type 1: _____

Question tag type 2: _____

Yes / No question: _____

15. Sara had sent out <u>more than 300</u> applications before she found a position.

Wh-question: _____

Question tag type 1: _____

Question tag type 2: _____

Yes / No question: _____

16. Jared had been to <u>more than 10</u> doctors before he found one he trusted.

Wh-question: _____

Question tag type 1: _____

Question tag type 2: _____

Yes / No question: _____

UNIT 7 | QUESTIONS IN THE PAST PERFECT

17. The kids had been in class <u>for over three hours</u> before the teacher arrived.

Wh-question: _____
Question tag type 1: _____
Question tag type 2: _____
Yes / No question: _____

18. We had visited <u>more than a dozen</u> schools before we finally found the right one for our daughter.

Wh-question: _____
Question tag type 1: _____
Question tag type 2: _____
Yes / No question: _____

19. The doubles team had already been on the tennis court <u>for two hours</u> when Samir and Nabil arrived.

Wh-question: _____
Question tag type 1: _____
Question tag type 2: _____
Yes / No question: _____

20. Richard had spoken <u>to the board of directors</u> before he resigned as CFO.

Wh-question: _____
Question tag type 1: _____
Question tag type 2: _____
Yes / No question: _____

21. Khalid had practiced his job interview <u>ten times</u> before he went in for the real thing.

Wh-question: _____
Question tag type 1: _____
Question tag type 2: _____
Yes / No question: _____

22. Half of the guests had already left before the party ended.

Wh-question: _____
Question tag type 1: _____
Question tag type 2: _____
Yes / No question: _____

23. Carol had already sold five pieces of jewelry by the time Tina was finishing her first sale of the day.

Wh-question: _____
Question tag type 1: _____
Question tag type 2: _____
Yes / No question: _____

24. Helga had looked at 50 houses before she finally found one she liked.

Wh-question: _____
Question tag type 1: _____
Question tag type 2: _____
Yes / No question: _____

25. Nina had eaten all the food by the time we got to the table.

Wh-question: _____
Question tag type 1: _____
Question tag type 2: _____
Yes / No question: _____

26. Carrie and Henry had known each other for nine years before they got married.

Wh-question: _____
Question tag type 1: _____
Question tag type 2: _____
Yes / No question: _____

UNIT 7 | QUESTIONS IN THE PAST PERFECT

27. Joyce had tucked her kids into bed two hours before the movie started.

Wh-question: _____
Question tag type 1: _____
Question tag type 2: _____
Yes / No question: _____

28. Robert had drunk most of the wine before the guests got there.

Wh-question: _____
Question tag type 1: _____
Question tag type 2: _____
Yes / No question: _____

29. Jason had bought the house six months before he got married.

Wh-question: _____
Question tag type 1: _____
Question tag type 2: _____
Yes / No question: _____

30. The company had warned Sylvia twice about tardiness before they fired her.

Wh-question: _____
Question tag type 1: _____
Question tag type 2: _____
Yes / No question: _____

31. Ahmed had visited Paris five times before he moved there.

Wh-question: _____
Question tag type 1: _____
Question tag type 2: _____
Yes / No question: _____

32. Martha had asked Bill out <u>four times</u> before she realized he didn't even like her.

Wh-question: _____

Question tag type 1: _____

Question tag type 2: _____

Yes / No question: _____

33. Todd had skipped classes <u>11 times</u> before the school suspended him.

Wh-question: _____

Question tag type 1: _____

Question tag type 2: _____

Yes / No question: _____

34. Mehran had left Palm Springs <u>three days</u> before spring break started.

Wh-question: _____

Question tag type 1: _____

Question tag type 2: _____

Yes / No question: _____

35. Joe had taken the dog out for a walk <u>twice</u> before the family went to bed.

Wh-question: _____

Question tag type 1: _____

Question tag type 2: _____

Yes / No question: _____

36. Carmen had already spent <u>90%</u> of her savings before she finished school.

Wh-question: _____

Question tag type 1: _____

Question tag type 2: _____

Yes / No question: _____

UNIT 7 | QUESTIONS IN THE PAST PERFECT

37. Gianni had spoken with <u>human resources</u> before he filed a complaint against his boss.

Wh-question: _____

Question tag type 1: _____

Question tag type 2: _____

Yes / No question: _____

38. Gina had studied law <u>for six years</u> before she passed the bar exam.

Wh-question: _____

Question tag type 1: _____

Question tag type 2: _____

Yes / No question: _____

39. Tracy had dated <u>six</u> different men before she found the right one.

Wh-question: _____

Question tag type 1: _____

Question tag type 2: _____

Yes / No question: _____

40. Meimei had patented <u>16</u> inventions before she turned 30.

Wh-question: _____

Question tag type 1: _____

Question tag type 2: _____

Yes / No question: _____

41. Bob and Alice had stayed <u>in a cabin with a dirt floor</u> before checking in at the hotel.

Wh-question: _____

Question tag type 1: _____

Question tag type 2: _____

Yes / No question: _____

42. Roger had lived in <u>ten</u> cities before he settled in San Francisco.

Wh-question: _____
Question tag type 1: _____
Question tag type 2: _____
Yes / No question: _____

43. Carlson had spoken <u>to his lawyers</u> before the trial began.

Wh-question: _____
Question tag type 1: _____
Question tag type 2: _____
Yes / No question: _____

44. I had spoken to the woman <u>several times</u> before we introducd ourselves.

Wh-question: _____
Question tag type 1: _____
Question tag type 2: _____
Yes / No question: _____

45. The witnesses had seen <u>an unknown man</u> at the crime scene before the police arrived.

Wh-question: _____
Question tag type 1: _____
Question tag type 2: _____
Yes / No question: _____

46. Before the exams started, school officials had warned students about <u>cheating</u>.

Wh-question: _____
Question tag type 1: _____
Question tag type 2: _____
Yes / No question: _____

UNIT 7 | QUESTIONS IN THE PAST PERFECT

47. <u>Jens</u> had turned on the alarm system before the doors automatically locked.

Wh-question: _____

Question tag type 1: _____

Question tag type 2: _____

Yes / No question: _____

48. Pirmin had already eaten <u>15</u> pieces of chocolate before his parents got home.

Wh-question: _____

Question tag type 1: _____

Question tag type 2: _____

Yes / No question: _____

49. <u>Ludmilla</u> had already left the office before the robbery occurred.

Wh-question: _____

Question tag type 1: _____

Question tag type 2: _____

Yes / No question: _____

50. The company had hired <u>45</u> employees before the new CEO took over.

Wh-question: _____

Question tag type 1: _____

Question tag type 2: _____

Yes / No question: _____

UNIT 8

QUESTIONS IN THE PAST PERFECT PROGRESSIVE

DIRECTIONS: Transform each of the following sentences into the type of question required in each of the given blanks. The underlined phrases in each sentence indicate which question phrase should be used.

Example:	Thales had been staring at the sky <u>for hours</u> before he saw the comet.
Wh-question:	How long had Thales been staring at the sky before he saw the comet?
Question tag type 1:	Thales had been staring at the sky for hours before he saw the comet, hadn't he? [expected positive response]
Question tag type 2:	Thales hadn't been staring at the sky for hours before he saw the comet, had he? [expected negative response]
Yes / No question:	Had Thales been staring at the sky for hours before he saw the comet?

1. I had been living in Rome <u>for 15 years</u> before I moved back to California.

Wh-question: _____

Question tag type 1: _____

Question tag type 2: _____

Yes / No question: _____

UNIT 8 | QUESTIONS IN THE PAST PERFECT PROGRESSIVE

2. I had been living <u>in Rome</u> for 15 years before I moved back to California.

Wh-question: _____

Question tag type 1: _____

Question tag type 2: _____

Yes / No question: _____

3. Samantha had been <u>making breakfast</u> just before the earthquake struck.

Wh-question: _____

Question tag type 1: _____

Question tag type 2: _____

Yes / No question: _____

4. Christos had been working <u>in the Caribbean</u> the year before he got married.

Wh-question: _____

Question tag type 1: _____

Question tag type 2: _____

Yes / No question: _____

5. I had been playing cards <u>with my nephew</u> just before the siren went off.

Wh-question: _____

Question tag type 1: _____

Question tag type 2: _____

Yes / No question: _____

6. We had been <u>watching *The Wizard of Oz* with the children</u> before they fell asleep.

Wh-question: _____

Question tag type 1: _____

Question tag type 2: _____

Yes / No question: _____

7. My uncle had been looking for his wallet <u>for over two days</u> before he finally found it.

Wh-question: _____

Question tag type 1: _____

Question tag type 2: _____

Yes / No question: _____

8. Giovanni had been swimming <u>for 30 minutes</u> when he realized he could no longer see land.

Wh-question: _____

Question tag type 1: _____

Question tag type 2: _____

Yes / No question: _____

9. René had been <u>working for a software company as a programmer</u> before going to work for Intel.

Wh-question: _____

Question tag type 1: _____

Question tag type 2: _____

Yes / No question: _____

10. Karen had been driving <u>an Italian sports car</u> before purchasing her dune buggy.

Wh-question: _____

Question tag type 1: _____

Question tag type 2: _____

Yes / No question: _____

11. Cynthia had been skiing <u>for 12 years</u> before she tried out for the Olympic team.

Wh-question: _____

Question tag type 1: _____

Question tag type 2: _____

Yes / No question: _____

12. Jimmy had been looking for employment <u>for over three years</u> before he found a job.

Wh-question: _____

Question tag type 1: _____

Question tag type 2: _____

Yes / No question: _____

13. Jean had been driving <u>for six hours straight</u> before she found a motel.

Wh-question: _____

Question tag type 1: _____

Question tag type 2: _____

Yes / No question: _____

14. Kenji and Keiko had been studying both English and Japanese <u>for two years</u> before they entered kindergarten.

Wh-question: _____

Question tag type 1: _____

Question tag type 2: _____

Yes / No question: _____

15. Michelle had been studying <u>at the Sorbonne</u> before going to Harvard to complete her PhD.

Wh-question: _____

Question tag type 1: _____

Question tag type 2: _____

Yes / No question: _____

16. Jean-Paul and Simone had been staying <u>at a hotel near the Piazza Navona</u> the week before we arrived.

Wh-question: _____

Question tag type 1: _____

Question tag type 2: _____

Yes / No question: _____

17. Tony had been arguing <u>with the manager</u> just before Ian walked into the room.

Wh-question: _____

Question tag type 1: _____

Question tag type 2: _____

Yes / No question: _____

18. David had been playing online games <u>all afternoon</u> when his computer crashed.

Wh-question: _____

Question tag type 1: _____

Question tag type 2: _____

Yes / No question: _____

19. <u>Over 200 people</u> had been working on the project when the money ran out.

Wh-question: _____

Question tag type 1: _____

Question tag type 2: _____

Yes / No question: _____

20. The staff had all been getting along <u>very nicely</u> before the new manager arrived.

Wh-question: _____

Question tag type 1: _____

Question tag type 2: _____

Yes / No question: _____

21. Elizabeth and John had been dating <u>for more than two years</u> when he finally proposed.

Wh-question: _____

Question tag type 1: _____

Question tag type 2: _____

Yes / No question: _____

UNIT 8 | QUESTIONS IN THE PAST PERFECT PROGRESSIVE

22. The young boy had been <u>trying to remove bread from the toaster</u> when he cut himself.

Wh-question: _____
Question tag type 1: _____
Question tag type 2: _____
Yes / No question: _____

23. Ted had been staying <u>with friends</u> before he bought a new house.

Wh-question: _____
Question tag type 1: _____
Question tag type 2: _____
Yes / No question: _____

24. Sally had been <u>ironing her shirt</u> just before the alarm sounded.

Wh-question: _____
Question tag type 1: _____
Question tag type 2: _____
Yes / No question: _____

25. Jenny had been playing basketball <u>every day</u> before she sprained her ankle.

Wh-question: _____
Question tag type 1: _____
Question tag type 2: _____
Yes / No question: _____

26. Heidi had been playing the violin for <u>more than four years</u> when she switched to the saxophone.

Wh-question: _____
Question tag type 1: _____
Question tag type 2: _____
Yes / No question: _____

27. The employees had been using the new software for two months when the upgrade came out.

Wh-question: _____
Question tag type 1: _____
Question tag type 2: _____
Yes / No question: _____

28. I had been living in the city for five years before I moved back to the country.

Wh-question: _____
Question tag type 1: _____
Question tag type 2: _____
Yes / No question: _____

29. Kim had been playing golf for six years before she turned pro.

Wh-question: _____
Question tag type 1: _____
Question tag type 2: _____
Yes / No question: _____

30. Carola had been living in Hampstead before she moved to Spain.

Wh-question: _____
Question tag type 1: _____
Question tag type 2: _____
Yes / No question: _____

31. We had been camping in the Crimea for two months before the Olympic games opened.

Wh-question: _____
Question tag type 1: _____
Question tag type 2: _____
Yes / No question: _____

UNIT 8 | QUESTIONS IN THE PAST PERFECT PROGRESSIVE

32. Emily had been <u>working as a wedding photographer</u> before she became a painter.

Wh-question: _____

Question tag type 1: _____

Question tag type 2: _____

Yes / No question: _____

33. The ship had been listing <u>for five hours</u> when the rescue team arrived.

Wh-question: _____

Question tag type 1: _____

Question tag type 2: _____

Yes / No question: _____

34. Jim had been eating <u>seafood</u> just before he fell ill.

Wh-question: _____

Question tag type 1: _____

Question tag type 2: _____

Yes / No question: _____

35. Leo had been playing soccer <u>in Barcelona</u> before he became a professional.

Wh-question: _____

Question tag type 1: _____

Question tag type 2: _____

Yes / No question: _____

36. Kerry had been paying <u>$5,000</u> in rent before he found a cheaper place.

Wh-question: _____

Question tag type 1: _____

Question tag type 2: _____

Yes / No question: _____

37. Bill had been working for the government <u>for 12 years</u> when he retired.

Wh-question: _____

Question tag type 1: _____

Question tag type 2: _____

Yes / No question: _____

38. Ron had been driving <u>for four hours</u> when he ran out of gas.

Wh-question: _____

Question tag type 1: _____

Question tag type 2: _____

Yes / No question: _____

39. Christine had been studying <u>statistics</u> before she switched to finance.

Wh-question: _____

Question tag type 1: _____

Question tag type 2: _____

Yes / No question: _____

40. Phyllis had been <u>walking</u> to work before she bought a bicycle.

Wh-question: _____

Question tag type 1: _____

Question tag type 2: _____

Yes / No question: _____

41. Jacob had been eating <u>in restaurants</u> before he learned to cook.

Wh-question: _____

Question tag type 1: _____

Question tag type 2: _____

Yes / No question: _____

UNIT 8 | QUESTIONS IN THE PAST PERFECT PROGRESSIVE

42. The postman had been standing <u>next to the ladder</u> just before it collapsed.

Wh-question: _____
Question tag type 1: _____
Question tag type 2: _____
Yes / No question: _____

43. Murphy had been feeling sick <u>for hours</u> before his family took him to the ER.

Wh-question: _____
Question tag type 1: _____
Question tag type 2: _____
Yes / No question: _____

44. Ms. Simms had been playing the lottery <u>for 20 years</u> before she hit the jackpot.

Wh-question: _____
Question tag type 1: _____
Question tag type 2: _____
Yes / No question: _____

45. The men had been filming <u>a desert scene</u> just before the UFO came into view.

Wh-question: _____
Question tag type 1: _____
Question tag type 2: _____
Yes / No question: _____

46. Babette had been cooking <u>crepes</u> just before the stove broke.

Wh-question: _____
Question tag type 1: _____
Question tag type 2: _____
Yes / No question: _____

47. Marcy had been working <u>as an attorney</u> the year before she became a professor.

Wh-question: _____

Question tag type 1: _____

Question tag type 2: _____

Yes / No question: _____

48. The two countries had been squabbling over <u>water rights</u> before they broke off talks.

Wh-question: _____

Question tag type 1: _____

Question tag type 2: _____

Yes / No question: _____

49. The guitarist had been playing <u>a jazz song</u> right before his E-string broke.

Wh-question: _____

Question tag type 1: _____

Question tag type 2: _____

Yes / No question: _____

50. Jacques had been <u>lifting heavy boxes</u> right before his back went out.

Wh-question: _____

Question tag type 1: _____

Question tag type 2: _____

Yes / No question: _____

UNIT 9

QUESTIONS IN THE FUTURE SIMPLE WITH WILL AND GOING TO

DIRECTIONS: Transform each of the following sentences into the type of question required in each of the given blanks. The underlined phrases in each sentence indicate which question phrase should be used.

Example:	*John will be there at 3 p.m.*
Wh-question:	*What time will John be there?*
Question tag type 1:	*John will be there at 3 p.m., won't he?* [expected positive response]
Question tag type 2:	*John won't be there at 3 p.m., will he?* [expected negative response]
Yes / No question:	*Will John be there at 3 p.m.?*

1. I'll be <u>at home</u> between 3:00 and 5:30 this afternoon.

Wh-question: _____

Question tag type 1: _____

Question tag type 2: _____

Yes / No question: _____

2. I'll be at home <u>between 9:00 and 11:00</u> tomorrow morning.

Wh-question: _____

Question tag type 1: _____

Question tag type 2: _____

Yes / No question: _____

3. We're going to go camping in Yosemite next summer.

Wh-question: _____

Question tag type 1: _____

Question tag type 2: _____

Yes / No question: _____

4. Tim's going to paint the kitchen yellow.

Wh-question: _____

Question tag type 1: _____

Question tag type 2: _____

Yes / No question: _____

5. More than 50 people will be at the party next week.

Wh-question: _____

Question tag type 1: _____

Question tag type 2: _____

Yes / No question: _____

6. Irene is going to help us with the catering.

Wh-question: _____

Question tag type 1: _____

Question tag type 2: _____

Yes / No question: _____

7. This time next week, I'll be in Paris.

Wh-question: _____

Question tag type 1: _____

Question tag type 2: _____

Yes / No question: _____

UNIT 9 | QUESTIONS IN THE FUTURE SIMPLE WITH WILL AND GOING TO   97

8. Martha is going to have her baby <u>in July</u>.

Wh-question: _____

Question tag type 1: _____

Question tag type 2: _____

Yes / No question: _____

9. I'm going to <u>take the train</u> to work tomorrow.

Wh-question: _____

Question tag type 1: _____

Question tag type 2: _____

Yes / No question: _____

10. <u>Martin</u> is going to help the kids with their homework next week.

Wh-question: _____

Question tag type 1: _____

Question tag type 2: _____

Yes / No question: _____

11. We're going to take <u>the Pacific route</u> to India.

Wh-question: _____

Question tag type 1: _____

Question tag type 2: _____

Yes / No question: _____

12. <u>Caroline</u> will help the patient into the van.

Wh-question: _____

Question tag type 1: _____

Question tag type 2: _____

Yes / No question: _____

13. You'll recognize me <u>by the red shirt and green socks I'll be wearing</u>.

Wh-question: _____

Question tag type 1: _____

Question tag type 2: _____

Yes / No question: _____

14. <u>Our neighbors</u> are going to help us with the cooking.

Wh-question: _____

Question tag type 1: _____

Question tag type 2: _____

Yes / No question: _____

15. The movie is going to start <u>in 10 minutes</u>.

Wh-question: _____

Question tag type 1: _____

Question tag type 2: _____

Yes / No question: _____

16. I'm going to take the car <u>to the Acme garage at the corner of 3rd St. and Maple</u>.

Wh-question: _____

Question tag type 1: _____

Question tag type 2: _____

Yes / No question: _____

17. We're going to leave the house <u>at 8:30</u> tomorrow morning.

Wh-question: _____

Question tag type 1: _____

Question tag type 2: _____

Yes / No question: _____

18. The dental bill will be more than $2,000.

Wh-question: _____
Question tag type 1: _____
Question tag type 2: _____
Yes / No question: _____

19. I'm going to be an organic chemist when I grow up.

Wh-question: _____
Question tag type 1: _____
Question tag type 2: _____
Yes / No question: _____

20. We'll have the results of your placement exam next Monday.

Wh-question: _____
Question tag type 1: _____
Question tag type 2: _____
Yes / No question: _____

21. The insurance representative is going to speak to the owners about replacing the stolen artwork.

Wh-question: _____
Question tag type 1: _____
Question tag type 2: _____
Yes / No question: _____

22. Sharon and Carl are going to name their son "Abraham."

Wh-question: _____
Question tag type 1: _____
Question tag type 2: _____
Yes / No question: _____

23. The host will dismiss the guests <u>at 11 p.m.</u>

Wh-question: _____

Question tag type 1: _____

Question tag type 2: _____

Yes / No question: _____

24. The weather on Saturday is going to be <u>nice and sunny</u>.

Wh-question: _____

Question tag type 1: _____

Question tag type 2: _____

Yes / No question: _____

25. I'm going to approach this delicate topic <u>in the most diplomatic way possible</u>.

Wh-question: _____

Question tag type 1: _____

Question tag type 2: _____

Yes / No question: _____

26. We're going to invite <u>more than 100</u> people to Maggie's wedding.

Wh-question: _____

Question tag type 1: _____

Question tag type 2: _____

Yes / No question: _____

27. They're going to demolish the old Jefferson Hotel <u>next year</u>.

Wh-question: _____

Question tag type 1: _____

Question tag type 2: _____

Yes / No question: _____

UNIT 9 | QUESTIONS IN THE FUTURE SIMPLE WITH WILL AND GOING TO

28. The plane will arrive at Heathrow shortly after noon.

Wh-question: _____

Question tag type 1: _____

Question tag type 2: _____

Yes / No question: _____

29. I'll be 31 years old this year.

Wh-question: _____

Question tag type 1: _____

Question tag type 2: _____

Yes / No question: _____

30. The president will visit four Asian capitals during his trip.

Wh-question: _____

Question tag type 1: _____

Question tag type 2: _____

Yes / No question: _____

31. The tickets for the concert will go on sale next weekend.

Wh-question: _____

Question tag type 1: _____

Question tag type 2: _____

Yes / No question: _____

32. I'll have a large lemonade to drink.

Wh-question: _____

Question tag type 1: _____

Question tag type 2: _____

Yes / No question: _____

33. Janet is going to lock the office at 5:15 p.m.

Wh-question: _____
Question tag type 1: _____
Question tag type 2: _____
Yes / No question: _____

34. Stephanie is going to major in business administration.

Wh-question: _____
Question tag type 1: _____
Question tag type 2: _____
Yes / No question: _____

35. Marion is going to have Chinese food for lunch.

Wh-question: _____
Question tag type 1: _____
Question tag type 2: _____
Yes / No question: _____

36. I'm going to ask the director about the company's new hiring policy.

Wh-question: _____
Question tag type 1: _____
Question tag type 2: _____
Yes / No question: _____

37. The school is going to need six drivers for the outing.

Wh-question: _____
Question tag type 1: _____
Question tag type 2: _____
Yes / No question: _____

38. Tracy and Donald are going to buy their daughter a zoology encyclopedia for her graduation.

Wh-question: _____

Question tag type 1: _____

Question tag type 2: _____

Yes / No question: _____

39. I'll be in the library if you need me.

Wh-question: _____

Question tag type 1: _____

Question tag type 2: _____

Yes / No question: _____

40. Teresa and Pauli are going to go with me to the opera this coming Tuesday.

Wh-question: _____

Question tag type 1: _____

Question tag type 2: _____

Yes / No question: _____

41. The director is going to say that he disagrees with your proposal.

Wh-question: _____

Question tag type 1: _____

Question tag type 2: _____

Yes / No question: _____

42. We'll need another week to finish writing the contract.

Wh-question: _____

Question tag type 1: _____

Question tag type 2: _____

Yes / No question: _____

43. They're going to need <u>three</u> additional cooks for the dinner party.

Wh-question: _____

Question tag type 1: _____

Question tag type 2: _____

Yes / No question: _____

44. <u>Vanessa</u> will assist you with your job application.

Wh-question: _____

Question tag type 1: _____

Question tag type 2: _____

Yes / No question: _____

45. I'm going to <u>use earplugs</u> to combat the noise.

Wh-question: _____

Question tag type 1: _____

Question tag type 2: _____

Yes / No question: _____

46. <u>Dorothy, Mark, Bob, and Edith</u> are going to go kayaking in Minnesota.

Wh-question: _____

Question tag type 1: _____

Question tag type 2: _____

Yes / No question: _____

47. Claudine is going to cook <u>spaghetti</u> for dinner tonight.

Wh-question: _____

Question tag type 1: _____

Question tag type 2: _____

Yes / No question: _____

48. David is going to take these old newspapers to the recycling bin.

Wh-question: _____

Question tag type 1: _____

Question tag type 2: _____

Yes / No question: _____

49. I'm going to call the police about the noisy neighbors.

Wh-question: _____

Question tag type 1: _____

Question tag type 2: _____

Yes / No question: _____

50. Grace is going to send her daughter to Cambridge to study English.

Wh-question: _____

Question tag type 1: _____

Question tag type 2: _____

Yes / No question: _____

UNIT 10

QUESTIONS IN THE FUTURE PROGRESSIVE WITH WILL AND GOING TO

DIRECTIONS: Transform each of the following sentences into the type of question required in each of the given blanks. The underlined phrases in each sentence indicate which question phrase should be used.

Example:	Sam will be leaving the house <u>at noon</u>.
Wh-question:	When will Sam be leaving the house?
Question tag type 1:	Sam will be leaving the house at noon, won't he? [expected positive response]
Question tag type 2:	Sam won't be leaving the house at noon, will he? [expected negative response]
Yes / No question:	Will Sam be leaving the house at noon?

1. The plane will be cruising <u>at an altitude of 10,000 m</u>.

Wh-question: _____

Question tag type 1: _____

Question tag type 2: _____

Yes / No question: _____

2. We'll be sitting <u>on the left facing the band</u>.

Wh-question: _____

Question tag type 1: _____

Question tag type 2: _____

Yes / No question: _____

UNIT 10 | QUESTIONS IN THE FUTURE PROGRESSIVE WITH WILL AND GOING TO

3. I'll be having dinner <u>with my ex-boyfriend</u> tomorrow night.

Wh-question: _____
Question tag type 1: _____
Question tag type 2: _____
Yes / No question: _____

4. Rowland and his wife are going to be <u>driving across the United States</u> next summer.

Wh-question: _____
Question tag type 1: _____
Question tag type 2: _____
Yes / No question: _____

5. We're going to be spending Christmas vacation <u>with my parents</u>.

Wh-question: _____
Question tag type 1: _____
Question tag type 2: _____
Yes / No question: _____

6. Henry will be visiting the United Arab Emirates <u>for three weeks</u>.

Wh-question: _____
Question tag type 1: _____
Question tag type 2: _____
Yes / No question: _____

7. He'll be staying <u>at the Intercontinental</u> in Dubai.

Wh-question: _____
Question tag type 1: _____
Question tag type 2: _____
Yes / No question: _____

8. Linda is going to be visiting her aunt in Boston.

Wh-question: _____

Question tag type 1: _____

Question tag type 2: _____

Yes / No question: _____

9. Donna is going to be camping with her cousins next summer.

Wh-question: _____

Question tag type 1: _____

Question tag type 2: _____

Yes / No question: _____

10. Susan and Felix are going to be lecturing at Oxford next semester.

Wh-question: _____

Question tag type 1: _____

Question tag type 2: _____

Yes / No question: _____

11. Eric will be sailing across the Atlantic one year from today.

Wh-question: _____

Question tag type 1: _____

Question tag type 2: _____

Yes / No question: _____

12. Mehdi is going to be retiring in two years.

Wh-question: _____

Question tag type 1: _____

Question tag type 2: _____

Yes / No question: _____

UNIT 10 | QUESTIONS IN THE FUTURE PROGRESSIVE WITH WILL AND GOING TO

13. The head of our department will be entertaining <u>more than 30 guests</u> next weekend.

Wh-question: _____
Question tag type 1: _____
Question tag type 2: _____
Yes / No question: _____

14. We will be landing <u>in approximately 30 minutes</u>.

Wh-question: _____
Question tag type 1: _____
Question tag type 2: _____
Yes / No question: _____

15. Professor Zhou will be conferencing with students <u>all day tomorrow</u>.

Wh-question: _____
Question tag type 1: _____
Question tag type 2: _____
Yes / No question: _____

16. <u>Janice</u> will be looking after the kids until we're back.

Wh-question: _____
Question tag type 1: _____
Question tag type 2: _____
Yes / No question: _____

17. Zheng is going to be studying <u>in Los Angeles</u> in the fall.

Wh-question: _____
Question tag type 1: _____
Question tag type 2: _____
Yes / No question: _____

18. Midori is going to be performing the Sibelius violin concerto this evening.

Wh-question: _____

Question tag type 1: _____

Question tag type 2: _____

Yes / No question: _____

19. More than four million people will be preparing for IELTS and Cambridge exams this year.

Wh-question: _____

Question tag type 1: _____

Question tag type 2: _____

Yes / No question: _____

20. I'm going to be taking my driving exam at 2:00 this afternoon.

Wh-question: _____

Question tag type 1: _____

Question tag type 2: _____

Yes / No question: _____

21. We're going to be subletting the house to an old friend of ours.

Wh-question: _____

Question tag type 1: _____

Question tag type 2: _____

Yes / No question: _____

22. I'll be celebrating New Year's Eve with my family.

Wh-question: _____

Question tag type 1: _____

Question tag type 2: _____

Yes / No question: _____

23. Patricia is going to be swimming for two more hours.

Wh-question: _____
Question tag type 1: _____
Question tag type 2: _____
Yes / No question: _____

24. Our company is going to be relocating to Singapore next year.

Wh-question: _____
Question tag type 1: _____
Question tag type 2: _____
Yes / No question: _____

25. I'll be needing the computer for at least another hour.

Wh-question: _____
Question tag type 1: _____
Question tag type 2: _____
Yes / No question: _____

26. Our team will be using a sequencer to analyze the DNA.

Wh-question: _____
Question tag type 1: _____
Question tag type 2: _____
Yes / No question: _____

27. Kathy will be spending the night on the Isle of Wight.

Wh-question: _____
Question tag type 1: _____
Question tag type 2: _____
Yes / No question: _____

28. The company is going to be hiring 30 more staff members in June.

Wh-question: _____
Question tag type 1: _____
Question tag type 2: _____
Yes / No question: _____

29. The committee is going to be holding its meetings in the upstairs conference room.

Wh-question: _____
Question tag type 1: _____
Question tag type 2: _____
Yes / No question: _____

30. They will be interviewing 15 more applicants.

Wh-question: _____
Question tag type 1: _____
Question tag type 2: _____
Yes / No question: _____

31. I'm going to be using this metal box to hold SD cards.

Wh-question: _____
Question tag type 1: _____
Question tag type 2: _____
Yes / No question: _____

32. We're going to be heading out for Las Vegas at 5 a.m.

Wh-question: _____
Question tag type 1: _____
Question tag type 2: _____
Yes / No question: _____

UNIT 10 | QUESTIONS IN THE FUTURE PROGRESSIVE WITH WILL AND GOING TO

33. The police will be issuing a statement to the press <u>tomorrow morning</u>.

Wh-question: _____

Question tag type 1: _____

Question tag type 2: _____

Yes / No question: _____

34. We'll be traveling to Scotland next month <u>by train</u>.

Wh-question: _____

Question tag type 1: _____

Question tag type 2: _____

Yes / No question: _____

35. I'll be <u>swimming in the Bahamas</u> at this exact time next week.

Wh-question: _____

Question tag type 1: _____

Question tag type 2: _____

Yes / No question: _____

36. The president and the board of directors are going to be discussing <u>company benefits</u> at the meeting.

Wh-question: _____

Question tag type 1: _____

Question tag type 2: _____

Yes / No question: _____

37. Tara's class is going to be studying <u>the future progressive verb tense</u> next week.

Wh-question: _____

Question tag type 1: _____

Question tag type 2: _____

Yes / No question: _____

38. The chemistry department will be scheduling final exams <u>during the last two weeks of the semester</u>.

Wh-question: _____
Question tag type 1: _____
Question tag type 2: _____
Yes / No question: _____

39. Ryuichi is going to be practicing the piano <u>from 7:00 to 9:00 this evening</u>.

Wh-question: _____
Question tag type 1: _____
Question tag type 2: _____
Yes / No question: _____

40. <u>Ahmed</u> is going to be taking care of my fish while I'm away.

Wh-question: _____
Question tag type 1: _____
Question tag type 2: _____
Yes / No question: _____

41. The children will be wanting their nap <u>in about an hour</u>.

Wh-question: _____
Question tag type 1: _____
Question tag type 2: _____
Yes / No question: _____

42. The workers will be harvesting grapes <u>the traditional way</u>.

Wh-question: _____
Question tag type 1: _____
Question tag type 2: _____
Yes / No question: _____

UNIT 10 | QUESTIONS IN THE FUTURE PROGRESSIVE WITH WILL AND GOING TO

43. Taehyon will be focusing on the housing market during his talk.

Wh-question: _____

Question tag type 1: _____

Question tag type 2: _____

Yes / No question: _____

44. I'll be wearing jeans, a plaid shirt, and a baseball cap.

Wh-question: _____

Question tag type 1: _____

Question tag type 2: _____

Yes / No question: _____

45. Andrew will be showing the new teaching assistants around campus.

Wh-question: _____

Question tag type 1: _____

Question tag type 2: _____

Yes / No question: _____

46. The directors will be talking to the new employees about company retirement plans.

Wh-question: _____

Question tag type 1: _____

Question tag type 2: _____

Yes / No question: _____

47. The guests will be paying by credit card.

Wh-question: _____

Question tag type 1: _____

Question tag type 2: _____

Yes / No question: _____

48. The kids will most likely be <u>playing video games</u> when we get home.

Wh-question: _____

Question tag type 1: _____

Question tag type 2: _____

Yes / No question: _____

49. I'm going to be taking my first flying lesson <u>this afternoon</u>.

Wh-question: _____

Question tag type 1: _____

Question tag type 2: _____

Yes / No question: _____

50. The authorities will be explaining <u>details of public emergency procedures</u> tonight.

Wh-question: _____

Question tag type 1: _____

Question tag type 2: _____

Yes / No question: _____

UNIT 11

QUESTIONS IN THE FUTURE PERFECT

DIRECTIONS: Transform each of the following sentences into the type of question required in each of the given blanks. The underlined phrases in each sentence indicate which question phrase should be used.

Example: Bob and Anne will have finished the preparations <u>by early evening</u>.

Wh-question: When will Bob and Anne have finished the preparations?

Question tag type 1: Bob and Anne will have finished the preparations by early evening, won't they? [expected positive response]

Question tag type 2: Bob and Anne won't have finished the preparations by early evening, will they? [expected negative response]

Yes / No question: Will Bob and Anne have finished the preparations by early evening?

1. Ingrid will have completed the project <u>by Friday evening</u>.

Wh-question: _____

Question tag type 1: _____

Question tag type 2: _____

Yes / No question: _____

2. At the end of this semester, I'll have studied English for six years.

Wh-question: _____

Question tag type 1: _____

Question tag type 2: _____

Yes / No question: _____

3. By 9 p.m. the full moon will have appeared in the sky.

Wh-question: _____

Question tag type 1: _____

Question tag type 2: _____

Yes / No question: _____

4. Tatiana and Dana will have come to a decision by 6 p.m.

Wh-question: _____

Question tag type 1: _____

Question tag type 2: _____

Yes / No question: _____

5. Andreas will have arrived in Russia by Tuesday of next week.

Wh-question: _____

Question tag type 1: _____

Question tag type 2: _____

Yes / No question: _____

6. Serena will have completed her homework by 10 p.m.

Wh-question: _____

Question tag type 1: _____

Question tag type 2: _____

Yes / No question: _____

UNIT 11 | QUESTIONS IN THE FUTURE PERFECT

7. I will have spoken to Mary's parents <u>by the weekend</u>.

Wh-question: _____
Question tag type 1: _____
Question tag type 2: _____
Yes / No question: _____

8. Gabrielle will have worked in <u>nine</u> different countries by the time she is 50.

Wh-question: _____
Question tag type 1: _____
Question tag type 2: _____
Yes / No question: _____

9. By this coming November, Angela will have worked in London <u>a full year</u>.

Wh-question: _____
Question tag type 1: _____
Question tag type 2: _____
Yes / No question: _____

10. June and Kerry will have completed the schedule <u>by the end of the day</u>.

Wh-question: _____
Question tag type 1: _____
Question tag type 2: _____
Yes / No question: _____

11. Susan will have written <u>11</u> books by the end of this year.

Wh-question: _____
Question tag type 1: _____
Question tag type 2: _____
Yes / No question: _____

12. My uncle will have been in the diplomatic service for over 50 years when he retires.

Wh-question: _____

Question tag type 1: _____

Question tag type 2: _____

Yes / No question: _____

13. By the time she's 21, Lucienne will have visited 65 countries.

Wh-question: _____

Question tag type 1: _____

Question tag type 2: _____

Yes / No question: _____

14. More than five million people will have seen the video by the weekend.

Wh-question: _____

Question tag type 1: _____

Question tag type 2: _____

Yes / No question: _____

15. By the end of this exercise, I will have formed 100 questions in the future perfect.

Wh-question: _____

Question tag type 1: _____

Question tag type 2: _____

Yes / No question: _____

16. Three million people will have visited the exhibit by the time it closes.

Wh-question: _____

Question tag type 1: _____

Question tag type 2: _____

Yes / No question: _____

UNIT 11 | QUESTIONS IN THE FUTURE PERFECT

17. The telescope will have made <u>10 million</u> images of deep space by January.

Wh-question: _____
Question tag type 1: _____
Question tag type 2: _____
Yes / No question: _____

18. At the end of this concert, Isaac will have performed this piece <u>a record 500 times</u>.

Wh-question: _____
Question tag type 1: _____
Question tag type 2: _____
Yes / No question: _____

19. By sunset, George will have walked <u>25</u> miles.

Wh-question: _____
Question tag type 1: _____
Question tag type 2: _____
Yes / No question: _____

20. If she makes it to the pier, Natasha will have swum <u>40</u> miles.

Wh-question: _____
Question tag type 1: _____
Question tag type 2: _____
Yes / No question: _____

21. By the end of this opera season, I'll have seen *Tristan und Isolde* <u>100</u> times.

Wh-question: _____
Question tag type 1: _____
Question tag type 2: _____
Yes / No question: _____

22. By the time we leave, Grandpa will have warned us about the dangers of government surveillance <u>20</u> times.

Wh-question: _____
Question tag type 1: _____
Question tag type 2: _____
Yes / No question: _____

23. By the time this administration is out of office, <u>dozens</u> of our civil liberties will have been overturned.

Wh-question: _____
Question tag type 1: _____
Question tag type 2: _____
Yes / No question: _____

24. Kathy will have been a teacher here <u>for 25 years</u> at the end of the current school year.

Wh-question: _____
Question tag type 1: _____
Question tag type 2: _____
Yes / No question: _____

25. By the end of this decade, <u>all</u> elephants will have been brutally slaughtered for their ivory.

Wh-question: _____
Question tag type 1: _____
Question tag type 2: _____
Yes / No question: _____

UNIT 12

QUESTIONS IN THE FUTURE PERFECT PROGRESSIVE

DIRECTIONS: Transform each of the following sentences into the type of question required in each of the given blanks. The underlined phrases in each sentence indicate which question phrase should be used.

Example: Soren will have been studying math <u>for five years</u> by the end of this month.
Wh-question: How long will Soren have been studying math by the end of this month?
Question tag type 1: Soren will have been studying math for five years by the end of this month, won't he? [expected positive response]
Question tag type 2: Soren won't have been studying math for five years by the end of this month, will he? [expected negative response]
Yes / No question: Will Soren have been studying math for five years by the end of this month?

1. At the end of today, Daisuke's class will have been working on English questions <u>for two weeks</u>.

Wh-question: _____
Question tag type 1: _____
Question tag type 2: _____
Yes / No question: _____

2. By the end of this semester, my brother will have been living in Hong Kong for 11 years.

Wh-question: _____

Question tag type 1: _____

Question tag type 2: _____

Yes / No question: _____

3. By the time Helen finishes school, she'll have been performing professionally for three years.

Wh-question: _____

Question tag type 1: _____

Question tag type 2: _____

Yes / No question: _____

4. By the time she's 20, Marika will have been playing soccer for 16 years.

Wh-question: _____

Question tag type 1: _____

Question tag type 2: _____

Yes / No question: _____

5. When he retires at 65, Woo-Young will have been teaching for over 30 years.

Wh-question: _____

Question tag type 1: _____

Question tag type 2: _____

Yes / No question: _____

6. On their next anniversary, my great-grandparents will have been married for 65 years.

Wh-question: _____

Question tag type 1: _____

Question tag type 2: _____

Yes / No question: _____

UNIT 12 | QUESTIONS IN THE FUTURE PERFECT PROGRESSIVE

7. In January, Hiroaki and Kyoko will have been dating <u>for three years</u>.

   Wh-question: _____
   Question tag type 1: _____
   Question tag type 2: _____
   Yes / No question: _____

8. When they finally reach their destination, Fred and Jennifer will have been driving <u>for one full day</u>.

   Wh-question: _____
   Question tag type 1: _____
   Question tag type 2: _____
   Yes / No question: _____

9. By the end of this month, the construction company will have been working on this building <u>for a full year</u>.

   Wh-question: _____
   Question tag type 1: _____
   Question tag type 2: _____
   Yes / No question: _____

10. By his birthday, Oscar will have been looking for work <u>for two years</u>.

    Wh-question: _____
    Question tag type 1: _____
    Question tag type 2: _____
    Yes / No question: _____

11. By the time she leaves, Kate will have been sitting at the computer <u>for nine hours</u>.

    Wh-question: _____
    Question tag type 1: _____
    Question tag type 2: _____
    Yes / No question: _____

12. By nighttime, the search team will have been looking for the hikers for 20 straight hours.

Wh-question: _____

Question tag type 1: _____

Question tag type 2: _____

Yes / No question: _____

13. When he turns 30, Pjotr will have been working as a dentist for two years.

Wh-question: _____

Question tag type 1: _____

Question tag type 2: _____

Yes / No question: _____

14. The opponents will have been debating this topic for more than a week when Parliament recesses.

Wh-question: _____

Question tag type 1: _____

Question tag type 2: _____

Yes / No question: _____

15. When the clock strikes midnight, they'll have been partying for 10 hours.

Wh-question: _____

Question tag type 1: _____

Question tag type 2: _____

Yes / No question: _____

16. At sundown, Nasser will have been fasting for 12 hours.

Wh-question: _____

Question tag type 1: _____

Question tag type 2: _____

Yes / No question: _____

UNIT 12 | QUESTIONS IN THE FUTURE PERFECT PROGRESSIVE

17. This trial will have been going on <u>for over a year</u> by the time a verdict is reached.

Wh-question: _____
Question tag type 1: _____
Question tag type 2: _____
Yes / No question: _____

18. By closing time, Keith and Andy will have been playing tennis <u>for over five hours</u>.

Wh-question: _____
Question tag type 1: _____
Question tag type 2: _____
Yes / No question: _____

19. By the time Penny finishes her degree, she'll have been studying Mandarin <u>for nine years</u>.

Wh-question: _____
Question tag type 1: _____
Question tag type 2: _____
Yes / No question: _____

20. On my parents' anniversary, my family will have been eating a completely vegetarian diet <u>for 10 years</u>.

Wh-question: _____
Question tag type 1: _____
Question tag type 2: _____
Yes / No question: _____

21. At the end of this month, Edward will have been working for the local government <u>for 20 years</u>.

Wh-question: _____
Question tag type 1: _____
Question tag type 2: _____
Yes / No question: _____

22. When Margaret retires, she will have been training horses for 15 years.

Wh-question: _____
Question tag type 1: _____
Question tag type 2: _____
Yes / No question: _____

23. At the one-hour mark, Joe will have been playing his guitar for four full hours.

Wh-question: _____
Question tag type 1: _____
Question tag type 2: _____
Yes / No question: _____

24. By winter, the construction workers will have been remodeling the house for six months.

Wh-question: _____
Question tag type 1: _____
Question tag type 2: _____
Yes / No question: _____

25. When she leaves Chicago in November, Vivian will have been working as a professional photographer for more than half of her life.

Wh-question: _____
Question tag type 1: _____
Question tag type 2: _____
Yes / No question: _____

SKELETAL FORMS OF QUESTIONS IN ALL ACTIVE TENSES

PRESENT SIMPLE

WH-SUBJECT QUESTIONS:

- with **be:**

    wh-question word (usually *who* or *what*) + is [+ complement / adverbial]

- with all other verbs:

    wh-question word (usually *who* or *what*) + base form of lexical verb+s [+ object / complement / adverbial]

WH-INFORMATION QUESTIONS:

- wh-question word or phrase + does + singular subject + base form of lexical verb [+ object / complement / adverbial]

- wh-question word or phrase + do + plural subject + base form of lexical verb [+ object / complement / adverbial]

TAG QUESTIONS TYPE I:

- with **be:**
    A) singular subject + is [+ complement / adverbial], + isn't + appropriate singular nominative pronoun
    B) plural subject + are [+ complement / adverbial], + aren't + appropriate plural nominative pronoun

TAG QUESTIONS TYPE I (continued):

- with all other verbs:
    A) singular subject + lexical verb+s [+ object / complement / adverbial], + doesn't + appropriate singular nominative pronoun

    B) plural subject + plural lexical verb [+ object / complement / adverbial], + don't + appropriate plural nominative pronoun

TAG QUESTIONS TYPE II:

- with **be**:
    A) singular subject + isn't [+ complement / adverbial], + is + appropriate singular nominative pronoun

    B) plural subject + aren't [+ complement / adverbial], + are + appropriate plural nominative pronoun

- with all other verbs:
    A) singular subject + doesn't + base form of lexical verb [+ object / complement / adverbial], + does + appropriate singular nominative pronoun

    B) plural subject + don't + base form of lexical verb [+ object / complement / adverbial], + do + appropriate plural nominative pronoun

YES / NO QUESTIONS:

- with **be**:
    A) is + singular subject [+ complement / adverbial]

    B) are + plural subject [+ complement / adverbial]

- with all other verbs:
    A) does + singular subject + base form of lexical verb [+ object / complement / adverbial]

    B) do + plural subject + base form of lexical verb [+ object / complement / adverbial]

Modal Verbs:

WH-SUBJECT QUESTIONS:

- wh-question word (usually *who* or *what*) + modal verb + base form of lexical verb [+ object / complement / adverbial]

WH-INFORMATION QUESTIONS:

- wh-question word or phrase + modal verb + subject + base form of lexical verb [+ object / complement / adverbial]

TAG QUESTIONS TYPE I:

- subject + modal verb + base form of lexical verb [+ object / complement / adverbial], + modal verb + not [normally contracted] + appropriate nominative pronoun

TAG QUESTIONS TYPE II:

- subject + modal verb + not [normally contracted] + base form of lexical verb [+ object / complement / adverbial], + modal verb + appropriate nominative pronoun

YES / NO QUESTIONS:

- modal verb + subject + lexical verb [+ object / complement / adverbial]

PRESENT PROGRESSIVE (CONTINUOUS)

WH-SUBJECT QUESTIONS:

- wh-question word (usually *who* or *what*) + is + lexical verb+ing [+ object / complement / adverbial]

WH-INFORMATION QUESTIONS:

A) wh-question word or phrase + is + singular subject + lexical verb+ing [+ object / complement / adverbial]

B) wh-question word or phrase + are + plural subject + lexical verb+ing [+ object / complement / adverbial]

TAG QUESTIONS TYPE I:

A) singular subject + is + lexical verb+ing [+ object / complement / adverbial], + isn't + appropriate singular nominative pronoun

B) plural subject + are + lexical verb+ing [+ object / complement / adverbial], + aren't + appropriate plural nominative pronoun

TAG QUESTIONS TYPE II:

    A) singular subject + isn't + lexical verb+ing [+ object / complement / adverbial], + is + appropriate singular nominative pronoun

    B) plural subject + aren't + lexical verb+ing [+ object / complement / adverbial], + are + appropriate plural nominative pronoun

YES / NO QUESTIONS:

    A) is + singular subject + verb+ing [+ object / complement / adverbial]

    B) are + plural subject + verb+ing [+ object / complement / adverbial]

Modal Verbs:

WH-SUBJECT QUESTIONS:

- wh-question word (usually who or what) + modal verb + be + lexical verb+ing [+ object / complement / adverbial]

WH-INFORMATION QUESTIONS:

- wh-question word or phrase + modal verb + subject + be + lexical verb+ing [+ object / complement / adverbial]

TAG QUESTIONS TYPE I:

- subject + modal verb + be + lexical verb+ing [+ object / complement / adverbial], + modal verb + not [normally contracted] + appropriate nominative pronoun

TAG QUESTIONS TYPE II:

- subject + modal verb + not [normally contracted] + be + lexical verb+ing [+ object / complement / adverbial], + modal verb + appropriate nominative pronoun

YES / NO QUESTIONS:

- modal verb + subject + be + lexical verb+ing [+ object / complement / adverbial]

SKELETAL FORMS OF QUESTIONS IN ALL ACTIVE TENSES

PRESENT PERFECT

WH-SUBJECT QUESTIONS:

- wh-question word (usually *who* or *what*) + has + past participle of lexical verb [+ object / complement / adverbial]

WH-INFORMATION QUESTIONS:

A) wh-question word or phrase + has + singular subject + past participle of lexical verb [+ object / complement / adverbial]

B) wh-question word or phrase + have + plural subject + past participle of lexical verb [+ object / complement / adverbial]

TAG QUESTIONS TYPE I:

A) singular subject + has + past participle of lexical verb [+ object / complement / adverbial], + hasn't + appropriate singular nominative pronoun

B) plural subject + have + past participle of lexical verb [+ object / complement / adverbial], + haven't + appropriate plural nominative pronoun

TAG QUESTIONS TYPE II:

A) singular subject + hasn't + past participle of lexical verb [+ object / complement / adverbial], + has + appropriate singular nominative pronoun

B) plural subject + haven't + past participle of lexical verb [+ object / complement / adverbial], + have + appropriate plural nominative pronoun

YES / NO QUESTIONS:

A) has + singular subject + past participle of lexical verb [+ object / complement / adverbial]

B) have + plural subject + past participle of lexical verb [+ object / complement / adverbial]

Modal Verbs:

WH-SUBJECT QUESTIONS:

- wh-question word (usually *who* or *what*) + modal verb + have + past participle of lexical verb [+ object / complement / adverbial]

WH-INFORMATION QUESTIONS:

- wh-question word or phrase + modal verb + subject + have + past participle of lexical verb [+ object / complement / adverbial]

TAG QUESTIONS TYPE I:

- subject + modal verb + have + past participle of lexical verb [+ object / complement / adverbial], + modal verb + not [normally contracted] + appropriate nominative pronoun

TAG QUESTIONS TYPE II:

- subject + modal verb + not [normally contracted] + have + past participle of lexical verb [+ object / complement / adverbial], + modal verb + appropriate nominative pronoun

YES / NO QUESTIONS:

- modal verb + subject + have + past participle of lexical verb [+ object / complement / adverbial]

PRESENT PERFECT PROGRESSIVE

WH-SUBJECT QUESTIONS:

- wh-question word (usually *who* or *what*) + has + been + lexical verb+ing [+ object / complement / adverbial]

WH-INFORMATION QUESTIONS:

A) wh-question word or phrase + has + singular subject + been + lexical verb+ing [+ object / complement / adverbial]

B) wh-question word or phrase + have + plural subject + been + lexical verb+ing [+ object / complement / adverbial]

TAG QUESTIONS TYPE I:

A) singular subject + has + been + lexical verb+ing [+ object / complement / adverbial], + hasn't + appropriate singular nominative pronoun

B) plural subject + have + been + lexical verb+ing [+ object / complement / adverbial], + haven't + appropriate plural nominative pronoun

TAG QUESTIONS TYPE II:

 A) singular subject + hasn't + been + lexical verb+ing [+ object / complement / adverbial], + has + appropriate singular nominative pronoun

 B) plural subject + haven't + been + lexical verb+ing [+ object / complement / adverbial], + have + appropriate plural nominative pronoun

YES / NO QUESTIONS:

 A) has + singular subject + been + lexical verb+ing [+ object / complement / adverbial]

 B) have + plural subject + been + lexical verb+ing [+ object / complement / adverbial]

Modal Verbs:

WH-SUBJECT QUESTIONS:

- wh-question word (usually *who* or *what*) + modal verb + have + been + lexical verb+ing [+ object / complement / adverbial]

WH-INFORMATION QUESTIONS:

- wh-question word or phrase + modal verb + subject + have + been + lexical verb+ing [+ object / complement / adverbial]

TAG QUESTIONS TYPE I:

- subject + modal verb + have + been + lexical verb+ing [+ object / complement / adverbial], + modal verb + not [normally contracted] + appropriate nominative pronoun

TAG QUESTIONS TYPE II:

- subject + modal verb + not [normally contracted] + have + been + lexical verb+ing [+ object / complement / adverbial], + modal verb + appropriate nominative pronoun

YES / NO QUESTIONS:

- modal verb + subject + have + been + lexical verb+ing [+ object / complement / adverbial]

SIMPLE PAST

WH-SUBJECT QUESTIONS:

- with **be**:

    wh-question word (usually *who* or *what*) + was [+ complement / adverbial]

- with all other verbs:

    wh-question word (usually *who* or *what*) + past tense of lexical verb [+ object / complement / adverbial]

TAG QUESTIONS TYPE I:

    A) singular subject + was [+ complement / adverbial], + wasn't + appropriate singular nominative pronoun

    B) plural subject + were [+ complement / adverbial], + weren't + appropriate singular nominative pronoun

TAG QUESTIONS TYPE II:

    A) singular subject + wasn't [+ complement / adverbial], + was + appropriate singular nominative pronoun

    B) plural subject + weren't [+ complement / adverbial], + were + appropriate singular nominative pronoun

YES / NO QUESTIONS:

    A) was + singular subject [+ complement / adverbial]

    B) were + plural subject [+ complement / adverbial]

WH-INFORMATION QUESTIONS:

    A) wh-question word or phrase + did + subject + base form of lexical verb [+ object / complement / adverbial]

TAG QUESTIONS TYPE I:

- subject + simple past form of lexical verb [+ object / complement / adverbial], + didn't + appropriate nominative pronoun

TAG QUESTIONS TYPE II:

- subject + didn't + base form of lexical verb [+ object / complement / adverbial], + did + appropriate nominative pronoun

YES / NO QUESTIONS:

- did + subject + base form of lexical verb [+ object / complement / adverbial]

PAST PROGRESSIVE

WH-SUBJECT QUESTIONS:

- with **be:**

    wh-question word (usually *who* or *what*) + was + being [+ complement / adverbial]

- with all other verbs:

    wh-question word (usually *who* or *what*) + was + lexical verb+ing [+ object / complement / adverbial]

WH-INFORMATION QUESTIONS:

A) wh-question word or phrase + was + singular subject + lexical verb+ing [+ object / complement / adverbial]

B) wh-question word or phrase + were + plural subject + lexical verb+ing [+ object / complement / adverbial]

TAG QUESTIONS TYPE I:

A) singular subject + was + lexical verb+ing [+ object / complement / adverbial], + wasn't + appropriate singular nominative pronoun

B) plural subject + were + lexical verb+ing [+ object / complement / adverbial], + weren't + appropriate plural nominative pronoun

TAG QUESTIONS TYPE II:

A) singular subject + wasn't + lexical verb+ing [+ object / complement / adverbial], + was + appropriate singular nominative pronoun

B) plural subject + weren't + lexical verb+ing [+ object / complement / adverbial], + were + appropriate plural nominative pronoun

YES / NO QUESTIONS:

   A) was + singular subject + lexical verb⁺ing [+ object / complement / adverbial]

   B) were + plural subject + lexical verb⁺ing [+ object / complement / adverbial]

PAST PERFECT

WH-SUBJECT QUESTIONS:

- wh-question word (usually *who* or *what*) + had + past participle of lexical verb [+ object / complement / adverbial]

WH-INFORMATION QUESTIONS:

- wh-question word or phrase + had + subject + past participle of lexical verb [+ object / complement / adverbial]

TAG QUESTIONS TYPE I:

- subject + had + past participle of lexical verb [+ object / complement / adverbial], + hadn't + appropriate nominative pronoun

TAG QUESTIONS TYPE II:

- subject + hadn't + past participle of lexical verb [+ object / complement / adverbial], + had + appropriate nominative pronoun

YES / NO QUESTIONS:

- had + subject + past participle of lexical verb [+ object / complement / adverbial]

PAST PERFECT PROGRESSIVE

WH-SUBJECT QUESTIONS:

- wh-question word (usually *who* or *what*) + had + been + lexical verb⁺ing [+ object / complement / adverbial]

WH-INFORMATION QUESTIONS:

- wh-question word or phrase + had + subject + been + lexical verb+ing [+ object / complement / adverbial]

TAG QUESTIONS TYPE I:

- subject + had + been + lexical verb+ing [+ object / complement / adverbial], + hadn't + appropriate nominative pronoun

TAG QUESTIONS TYPE II:

- subject + hadn't + been + lexical verb+ing [+ object / complement / adverbial], + had + appropriate nominative pronoun

YES / NO QUESTIONS:

- had + subject + been + lexical verb+ing [+ object / complement / adverbial]

FUTURE SIMPLE WITH "WILL"

WH-SUBJECT QUESTIONS:

- wh-question word (usually *who* or *what*) + will + base form of lexical verb [+ object / complement / adverbial]

WH-INFORMATION QUESTIONS:

- wh-question word or phrase + will + subject + base form of lexical verb [+ object / complement / adverbial]

TAG QUESTIONS TYPE I:

- subject + will + base form of lexical verb [+ object / complement / adverbial], + won't + appropriate nominative pronoun

TAG QUESTIONS TYPE II:

- subject + won't + base form of lexical verb [+ object / complement / adverbial], + will + appropriate nominative pronoun

YES / NO QUESTIONS:

- will + subject + base form of lexical verb [+ object / complement / adverbial]

FUTURE SIMPLE WITH "GOING TO"

WH-SUBJECT QUESTIONS:

- wh-question word (usually *who* or *what*) + is + going to + base form of lexical verb [+ object / complement / adverbial]

WH-INFORMATION QUESTIONS:

A) wh-question word or phrase + is + singular subject + going to + base form of lexical verb [+ object / complement / adverbial]

B) wh-question word or phrase + are + plural subject + going to + base form of lexical verb [+ object / complement / adverbial]

TAG QUESTIONS TYPE I:

A) singular subject + is + going to + base form of lexical verb [+ object / complement / adverbial], + isn't + appropriate singular nominative pronoun

B) plural subject + are + going to + base form of lexical verb [+ object / complement / adverbial], + aren't + appropriate plural nominative pronoun

TAG QUESTIONS TYPE II:

A) singular subject + isn't + going to + base form of lexical verb [+ object / complement / adverbial], + is + appropriate singular nominative pronoun

B) plural subject + aren't + going to + base form of lexical verb [+ object / complement / adverbial], + are + appropriate plural nominative pronoun

YES / NO QUESTIONS:

A) is + singular subject + going to + base form of lexical verb [+ object / complement / adverbial]

B) are + plural subject + going to + base form of lexical verb [+ object / complement / adverbial]

SKELETAL FORMS OF QUESTIONS IN ALL ACTIVE TENSES

FUTURE PROGRESSIVE WITH "WILL"

WH-SUBJECT QUESTIONS:

- wh-question word (usually *who* or *what*) + will + be + lexical verb+ing [+ object / complement / adverbial]

WH-INFORMATION QUESTIONS:

- wh-question word or phrase + will + subject + be + lexical verb+ing [+ object / complement / adverbial]

TAG QUESTIONS TYPE I:

- subject + will + be + lexical verb+ing [+ object / complement / adverbial], won't + appropriate nominative pronoun

TAG QUESTIONS TYPE II:

- subject + won't + be + lexical verb+ing [+ object / complement / adverbial], will + appropriate nominative pronoun

YES / NO QUESTIONS:

- will + subject + be + lexical verb+ing [+ object / complement / adverbial]

FUTURE PROGRESSIVE WITH "GOING TO"

WH-SUBJECT QUESTIONS:

- wh-question word (usually *who* or *what*) + is + going to + be + lexical verb+ing [+ object / complement / adverbial]

WH-INFORMATION QUESTIONS:

- wh-question word or phrase + is + singular subject + going to + be + lexical verb+ing [+ object / complement / adverbial]
- wh-question word or phrase + are + plural subject + going to + be + lexical verb+ing [+ object / complement / adverbial]

TAG QUESTIONS TYPE I:

    A) singular subject + is + going to + be + lexical verb+ing [+ object / complement / adverbial], isn't + appropriate singular nominative pronoun

    B) plural subject + are + going to + be + lexical verb+ing [+ object / complement / adverbial], aren't + appropriate plural nominative pronoun

TAG QUESTIONS TYPE II:

    A) singular subject + isn't + going to + be + lexical verb+ing [+ object / complement / adverbial], is + appropriate singular nominative pronoun

    B) plural subject + aren't + going to + be + lexical verb+ing [+ object / complement / adverbial], are + appropriate singular nominative pronoun

YES / NO QUESTIONS:

    A) is + singular subject + going to + be + lexical verb+ing [+ object / complement / adverbial]

    B) are + plural subject + going to + be + lexical verb+ing [+ object / complement / adverbial]

FUTURE PERFECT WITH "WILL"

WH-SUBJECT QUESTIONS:

- wh-question word (usually *who* or *what*) + will + have + past participle of lexical verb [+ object / complement / adverbial]

WH-INFORMATION QUESTIONS:

- wh-question word or phrase + will + subject + have + past participle of lexical verb [+ object / complement / adverbial]

TAG QUESTIONS TYPE I:

- subject + will + have + past participle of lexical verb [+ object / complement / adverbial], won't + appropriate nominative pronoun

TAG QUESTIONS TYPE II:

- subject + won't + have + past participle of lexical verb [+ object / complement / adverbial], will + appropriate nominative pronoun

SKELETAL FORMS OF QUESTIONS IN ALL ACTIVE TENSES

YES / NO QUESTIONS:

- will + subject + have + past participle of lexical verb [+ object / complement / adverbial]

FUTURE PERFECT WITH "GOING TO"

WH-SUBJECT QUESTIONS:

- wh-question word (usually *who* or *what*) + is + going to + have + past participle of lexical verb [+ object / complement / adverbial]

WH-INFORMATION QUESTIONS:

A) wh-question word or phrase + is + singular subject + going to + have + past participle of lexical verb [+ object / complement / adverbial]

B) wh-question word or phrase + are + plural subject + going to + have + past participle of lexical verb [+ object / complement / adverbial]

TAG QUESTIONS TYPE I:

A) subject + is + going to + have + past participle of lexical verb [+ object / complement / adverbial], isn't + appropriate singular nominative pronoun

B) subject + are + going to + have + past participle of lexical verb [+ object / complement / adverbial], aren't + appropriate plural nominative pronoun

TAG QUESTIONS TYPE II:

A) subject + isn't + going to + have + past participle of lexical verb [+ object / complement / adverbial], is + appropriate singular nominative pronoun

B) subject + aren't + going to + have + past participle of lexical verb [+ object / complement / adverbial], are + appropriate plural nominative pronoun

YES / NO QUESTIONS:

A) is + singular subject + going to + have + past participle of lexical verb [+ object / complement / adverbial]

B) are + plural subject + going to + have + past participle of lexical verb [+ object / complement / adverbial]

FUTURE PERFECT PROGRESSIVE WITH "WILL"

WH-SUBJECT QUESTIONS:

- ◆ wh-question word (usually *who* or *what*) + will + have + been + lexical verb⁺ing [+ object / complement / adverbial]

WH-INFORMATION QUESTIONS:

- ◆ wh-question word or phrase + will + subject + have + been + lexical verb⁺ing [+ object / complement / adverbial]

TAG QUESTIONS TYPE I:

- ◆ subject + will + have + been + lexical verb⁺ing [+ object / complement / adverbial], + won't + appropriate nominative pronoun

TAG QUESTIONS TYPE II:

- ◆ subject + won't + have + been + lexical verb⁺ing [+ object / complement / adverbial], + will + appropriate nominative pronoun

YES / NO QUESTIONS:

- ◆ will + subject + have + been + lexical verb⁺ing [+ object / complement / adverbial]

FUTURE PERFECT PROGRESSIVE WITH "GOING TO"

WH-SUBJECT QUESTIONS:

- ◆ wh-question word (usually *who* or *what*) + is + going to + have + been + lexical verb⁺ing [+ object / complement / adverbial]

WH-INFORMATION QUESTIONS:

- A) wh-question word or phrase + is + singular subject + going to + have + been + lexical verb ⁺ing [+ object / complement / adverbial]
- B) wh-question word or phrase + are + plural subject + going to + have + been + lexical verb ⁺ing [+ object / complement / adverbial]

SKELETAL FORMS OF QUESTIONS IN ALL ACTIVE TENSES

TAG QUESTIONS TYPE I:

A) singular subject + is + going to + have + been + lexical verb⁺ing [+ object / complement / adverbial], isn't + appropriate singular nominative pronoun

B) plural subject + are + going to + have + been + lexical verb⁺ing [+ object / complement / adverbial], aren't + appropriate plural nominative pronoun

TAG QUESTIONS TYPE II:

A) singular subject + isn't + going to + have + been + lexical verb⁺ing [+ object / complement / adverbial], is + appropriate singular nominative pronoun

B) plural subject + aren't + going to + have + been + lexical verb⁺ing [+ object / complement / adverbial], are + appropriate plural nominative pronoun

YES / NO QUESTIONS:

A) is + singular subject + going to + have + been + lexical verb⁺ing [+ object / complement / adverbial]

B) are + plural subject + going to + have + been + lexical verb⁺ing [+ object / complement / adverbial]

ABOUT THE AUTHOR

JJ Polk, PhD, completed his post-doctoral teaching credentials in the UK with a UCLES Diploma. A former CELTA tutor and IELTS examiner, Polk has lived and taught in Europe, the Middle East, and the Far East. He now teaches at the University of Southern California in Los Angeles and is especially interested in interdisciplinary perspectives on pragmatics in communication.

www.ingramcontent.com/pod-product-compliance
Lightning Source LLC
Chambersburg PA
CBHW081358290426
44110CB00018B/2410